30 MINUTE MEALS

Easy Recipes for Complete Meals

INTRODUCTION

Does the idea of serving delicious, nutritious meals in only 30 minutes sound too good to be true? There is no doubt that today, more than ever before, it is important to make the most of our time in the kitchen. We live in an age where time is more precious than money. Many people spend twice as much money purchasing expensive gourmet carry-out and convenience foods in order to get a meal on the table fast. But, let's face it—a steady diet of take-out and frozen meals becomes monotonous after a while.

30 Minute Meals is one solution to the mealtime dilemma. This cookbook shows you how to streamline food preparation so that fast, appetizing and nutritious meals *can* fit into your busy schedule. Organization is the key to successful 30-minute cooking. Read on to discover shortcuts and tips that will help you get organized, as well as information to guide you through the meal plans that follow.

HOW THE MENU PLANS WORK

As you page through the publication, you'll see that each meal follows a menu format. Bold recipe titles in the menu indicate the recipes that are included in the publication; the other items are serving suggestions that can be purchased ready-made as an easy addition. Most of the menus contain three to four recipes: a main-dish, side-dish and dessert recipe and sometimes a beverage. Some menus include two side dishes along with the main dish, with a simple dessert idea provided as a suggestion. The first page of each chapter lists all the menus included in that chapter so you can easily see them at a glance.

Following the menu is the Game Plan or the blueprint to follow while preparing the meal. In order to complete the meal within 30 minutes, most of the dishes need to be prepared or cooked simultaneously. For example, while the meat is browning, vegetables can be chopped. Or dessert preparation can be started while a soup is simmering. The Game Plan outlines, step-by-step, the most time-efficient way to prepare the various recipes in the meal. *If you do not follow the Game Plan, the meals may take longer than 30 minutes to prepare.* The recipes listed in the menu and a color photograph of the meal accompany each Game Plan.

In devising these meals, no time has been allowed for distractions like answering phone calls, feeding the cat, attending to the kids or setting the table. If possible, talk someone else into handling these things for you.

The 30 minutes does *not* include assembling the ingredients or washing fruits and vegetables, meat, poultry and fish. If a recipe calls for an ingredient that is already cooked, such as "1 cup cooked rice," then time is not allowed for cooking. However, "1 cup rice, cooked" would include time for cooking. If you follow an ingredient substitution given with a recipe, such as substituting dried pasta for fresh, the cooking time may need to be increased.

A food processor or blender is needed for some of the recipes. A microwave oven, while helpful for many tasks, is *not* necessary to cook the meals in 30 minutes.

Recipes cooked on top of the stove were tested using gas burners, while oven-baked and broiled dishes were tested with electric ovens. Keep in mind that cooking times may vary because all ovens do not cook in exactly the same way.

Times may also vary because all people do not cook at the same speed. The meals are not difficult to prepare, but someone who is less skilled in cooking will require more time to complete them. In addition, it will be easier to complete a meal in the 30 minutes allotted when you prepare it for a second or third time and have become more familiar with the recipes.

TIME-SAVING SHORTCUTS

Cooking a meal from start to finish is possible in 30 minutes if you practice the following guidelines and time-saving shortcuts. The recipes and meals in this publication were designed with many of these shortcuts in mind.

▲ Keep your cupboards, refrigerator and freezer well-stocked with grocery staples and make sure your kitchen is equipped with basic cooking tools and utensils. (See pages 4–6 for lists of staples and basic kitchen equipment.)

▲ Always read the complete menu and all the recipes, then make a shopping list of any ingredients that you need.

▲ Read through the recipes a second time before starting to cook. Also read the Game Plan to see the order in which the recipes are prepared and if the oven or broiler needs preheating.

▲ There is no rule that says these meals must be prepared by only one person. Two people in the kitchen make the work go faster, plus it's more fun.

▲ Take advantage of cut-up raw vegetables available in the produce section or salad bar at the supermarket. These ready-to-use vegetables let you forego washing and chopping and are a great time-saver. Many supermarkets are now selling fresh ingredients prepared and packaged together for salads and one-dish meals as well.

▲ Look for presliced and diced fresh fruits available in the produce section of supermarkets to use in fruit salads and desserts—they're a nice alternative to canned fruits. Frozen fruits are another way to make a quick dessert. Most frozen fruits are better if served before they are completely thawed.

▲ Purchase cheese that has already been shredded or sliced. Supermarkets now carry a wide variety of prepared cheeses, including Cheddar, mozzarella and Swiss. This saves both preparation and cleanup time.

▲ Boneless chicken and turkey cook quickly and are available in ready-to-cook fillets, tenderloins, cutlets and nuggets. Both can also be purchased ground for use in stir-fries, burgers, meat loaves or meatballs.

▲ Beef kabobs are sold completely assembled in most supermarkets. They require only a glaze or marinade and a few minutes under the broiler before serving.

▲ Check your local supermarket bakery for pound cakes, angel food cakes, individual cake slices, brownies and cookies.

▲ If you have unexpected guests, pick up ready-made salads or other foods from the deli section of the supermarket. At home, add your own personal touch by incorporating some fresh ingredients, herbs and seasonings to give them extra crunch, color and flavor.

▲ Remember that smaller pieces of food cook faster than larger pieces, so taking a few extra minutes to cut vegetables, such as potatoes, can save time in the long run. Also keep in mind that thin cuts of meat cook more quickly than thick cuts.

▲ If you have a microwave oven, it can trim even more time off meal preparation. Use it for such tasks as thawing and cooking frozen foods, melting chocolate and butter and heating tortillas and other breads.

▲ Your freezer can be one of your best assets. When you have a bit more time to spend in the kitchen, prepare a double batch of whatever it is you're cooking for dinner—a spaghetti sauce, casserole, soup or stew—and freeze the leftovers in serving-size portions for super-quick meals later. If you want to save money on convenience foods, shred your own cheese or bone your own chicken breasts and freeze both for later use. Spending a few hours stockpiling your freezer with home-prepared foods yields big payoffs later in both time and money.

THE WELL-STOCKED KITCHEN

An organized kitchen that is well-stocked with grocery staples and basic kitchen equipment is essential to cooking efficiently. By keeping frequently used ingredients on hand in your cupboards, refrigerator and freezer, you make less trips to the grocery store and spend less time shopping when you're there. Likewise, the proper kitchen utensils and equipment will make life in the kitchen easier.

KITCHEN STAPLES

The following is a list of suggested staples to keep on hand. Most of the foods on this list are used in a number of these recipes; some are used only a few times but it makes sense to have them for use in other recipes as well. The perishable foods are called for often enough that it is a good idea to have them readily available. All of these staples can be purchased at larger supermarkets.

Dairy Products

butter (or margarine)
cheese: shredded Cheddar, cream cheese, grated Parmesan
eggs
half-and-half

ice cream
milk: fresh, sweetened condensed
plain yogurt
sour cream

Fruits *(all fruits are fresh unless indicated otherwise)*

apples
lemons
limes
oranges
pears (canned)
pineapple (canned)
strawberries (frozen)

Seasonings, Herbs & Spices *(all herbs are dried and spices are ground unless indicated otherwise)*

basil
bay leaves
black pepper
chili powder
cilantro (fresh)
cinnamon
cumin
dill weed
fennel seeds
ginger (fresh)
nutmeg
oregano
parsley: fresh, dried
poppy seeds
rosemary
red pepper (cayenne)
salt
sage
thyme

Oils & Vinegars

oils: olive, sesame, vegetable
vinegars: balsamic, seasoned rice, white wine

Pasta & Grains

cornmeal
flour, all-purpose
oats
rice

Sauces & Condiments

honey
hot pepper sauce
Italian dressing (bottled)
mayonnaise
mustard, Dijon-style
salsa
soy sauce

Vegetables *(all vegetables are fresh unless indicated otherwise)*

beans, canned: Great Northern, kidney, black beans
beans, green (frozen)
bell peppers: red, green or yellow
broccoli, chopped (frozen)
carrots
celery
chilies, chopped green (canned)
corn (frozen)
garlic
lettuce
onions: green, all-purpose
peas, green (frozen)
peppers, roasted red (bottled)
potatoes
spinach, chopped (frozen)
tomatoes: fresh, canned

Miscellaneous

baking powder
bread crumbs, seasoned dry
bread: French, pita
chicken breasts, boned and skinned
chicken broth
coconut, shredded

cornstarch
sugar: granulated, powdered
tortillas: flour, corn
tuna (canned)
vanilla extract
wine, dry white

KITCHEN UTENSILS

If you don't have the proper tools, food preparation takes more time. It also is a waste of time when you have to go searching for that proper tool. Cooking utensils should be organized so that they are within easy reach of where they will be needed, such as storing pots, pans, spatulas, slotted spoons and pot holders near the stove.

The basic utensils listed below are the essentials. Remember that keeping your cooking tools ready for action, such as knives that are sharpened, makes cooking go faster.

Knives and Spoons

8″ or 10″ chef's knife
2 paring knives
serrated bread knife

wooden spoons
slotted spoon

Pots, Pans, Casseroles and more

8-quart stockpot
8″ nonstick skillet with lid
10″ nonstick skillet with lid
1-, 2- and 3-quart saucepans with lids
steamer basket
baking sheet
12-cup muffin pan
shallow baking dish
1- and 2-quart casseroles with lids
set of measuring spoons
set of dry measuring cups
2-cup liquid measuring cup

wire whisk
electric hand mixer
food processor/blender
small, medium and large mixing bowl
pastry bag with large star tip
2 cooling racks
colander
spatulas (metal and plastic)
pastry brush
cutting boards
can opener
bottle opener
vegetable peeler

Practical Poultry

With today's trends toward lighter eating, cooking with poultry continues to gain in popularity. Try our zesty Chicken Fajitas, enticing Monterey Chicken Sandwich or impressive Turkey Cordon Bleu for starters.

Chicken-Asparagus Salad (page 26)

POULTRY - MENUS

Chicken Fajitas
Chunky Guacamole
Caramelized Pears
(pages 8-9)
▲

Monterey Chicken
Sandwiches
Corn-on-the-Cob
with Chili Butter
Raspberry Dessert Pizza
(pages 10-11)
▲

Creamy Herbed Chicken
Tomatoes Vinaigrette
Italian bread
Strawberry Dessert Loaf
(pages 12-14)
▲

Soft Turkey Tacos
Cheesy Refried Beans
Creamy Citrus Pie
(pages 15-17)
▲

Turkey Cordon Bleu
Calico Vegetable Sauté
Peachy Strawberry
Shortcake
(pages 18-19)
▲

Mini Turkey Loaves
Vegetable Stir-Fry
Creamy Mashed
Potatoes
Apple pie
(pages 20-21)
▲

Citrus Chicken
Poppy Seed Noodles
Garden Vegetable
Medley
Blueberry pie
(pages 22-23)
▲

Broiled Chicken Salad
Tortillas
Cherry Sundaes
(pages 24-25)
▲

Chicken-Asparagus
Salad
Sun-Dried Tomato
Muffins
Glazed Orange Slices
(pages 26-28)
▲

Bold titles indicate recipes included

Chicken Fajitas

Chunky Guacamole

Caramelized Pears

GAME PLAN

▲ **Cut vegetables and chicken for fajitas.**

▲ **Prepare Chunky Guacamole.**

▲ **Core and slice pears for dessert; cover and set aside.**

▲ **Finish Chicken Fajitas.**

▲ **Just before serving, finish Caramelized Pears.**

Chicken Fajitas

1 tablespoon vegetable oil
1 large green pepper, thinly sliced
1 large red pepper, thinly sliced
1 large onion, thinly sliced
1 clove garlic, minced
4 boneless, skinless chicken breast halves (about 1 pound), cut into ½-inch strips
½ teaspoon dried oregano leaves, crushed
2 tablespoons dry white wine or water
Salt and black pepper
8 (8-inch) flour tortillas

1. Heat oil in large skillet over medium-high heat. Add green and red peppers, onion and garlic. Cook 3 to 4 minutes or until crisp-tender, stirring occasionally. Remove vegetables with slotted spoon; set aside.

2. Add chicken and oregano to skillet. Cook 4 minutes or until chicken is no longer pink in center, stirring occasionally.

3. Return vegetables to skillet. Add wine. Season with salt and black pepper to taste; cover. Continue cooking 2 minutes or until thoroughly heated.

4. Meanwhile, warm tortillas (page 15). Fill tortillas with chicken mixture; serve with Chunky Guacamole.

Makes 4 servings

Chunky Guacamole

2 ripe avocados, pitted and peeled
¼ cup sour cream
¼ cup salsa

Place all ingredients in food processor or blender container; process briefly (small chunks should remain). Cover; refrigerate.

Makes 4 servings

Caramelized Pears

1 tablespoon butter
2 or 3 ripe pears, cored and thinly sliced
½ cup butterscotch-caramel-fudge topping
Scoops of vanilla ice cream

1. Melt butter in medium skillet over medium heat. Add pears. Cook 2 minutes or until pears are softened, stirring occasionally.

2. Add topping; heat until bubbly, stirring occasionally. Serve over ice cream.

Makes 4 servings

Top to bottom: Caramelized Pears, Chicken Fajitas, Chunky Guacamole

Monterey Chicken Sandwiches

Corn-on-the-Cob with Chili Butter

Raspberry Dessert Pizza

GAME PLAN

▲ **Preheat oven to 450°.**

▲ **Cook chicken.**

▲ **While chicken is cooking, slice onion and split rolls for sandwiches.**

▲ **Bake crust for Raspberry Dessert Pizza.**

▲ **While crust is baking, boil water for corn.**

▲ **Finish dessert.**

▲ **Cook corn.**

▲ **While corn is cooking, finish Monterey Chicken Sandwiches.**

▲ **Prepare Corn-on-the-Cob with Chili Butter.**

Left to right: Monterey Chicken Sandwich, Corn-on-the-Cob with Chili Butter

Monterey Chicken Sandwiches

1 tablespoon oil
1 tablespoon butter
4 boneless, skinless chicken breast halves (about 1 pound)
1 teaspoon dried thyme leaves, crushed
Salt and pepper
1 large red onion, thinly sliced
4 Kaiser rolls, split
Radicchio or lettuce leaves

1. Heat oil and butter in large skillet over medium heat. Add chicken; sprinkle with thyme. Cook 8 minutes or until browned on both sides and no longer pink in center, turning after 4 minutes. Season with salt and pepper to taste. Remove from skillet; keep warm.

2. Add onion to skillet; cook until tender.

3. Fill rolls with radicchio leaves, chicken and onions. Serve with mango chutney and olives, if desired.
Makes 4 sandwiches

Corn-on-the-Cob with Chili Butter

4 ears of corn
¼ cup butter, softened
1 tablespoon snipped fresh chives
1 teaspoon chili powder
Salt and pepper

1. Bring large pan of water to a boil. Add corn; boil 5 minutes.

2. Meanwhile, combine butter, chives and chili powder.

3. Remove corn from water; spread with butter mixture. Season with salt and pepper to taste.
Makes 4 servings

Raspberry Dessert Pizza

1 (9-inch) refrigerated pie crust
⅓ cup white chocolate chips
1 cup raspberry or blueberry pie filling

1. Preheat oven to 450°F.

2. Unfold pie crust; place on baking sheet. Bake 6 to 8 minutes or until golden brown.

3. Remove crust from oven; sprinkle with chips. Continue baking 1 minute or until chips are softened.

4. Spread chocolate with spatula to cover crust; top with pie filling. Cool before serving. Refrigerate leftovers.
Makes 6 to 8 servings

Refrigerate leftover pie filling. Use as a topping for ice cream or cake slices.

Creamy Herbed Chicken

Tomatoes Vinaigrette

Italian bread

Strawberry Dessert Loaf

GAME PLAN

▲ **Prepare Strawberry Dessert Loaf (page 14).**

▲ **Boil water for pasta.**

▲ **Cut vegetables for Creamy Herbed Chicken and Tomatoes Vinaigrette (page 14).**

▲ **Cut chicken.**

▲ **Finish Tomatoes Vinaigrette.**

▲ **Finish Creamy Herbed Chicken.**

Creamy Herbed Chicken

1 (9-ounce) package fresh bow tie pasta or fusilli
1 tablespoon vegetable oil
4 boneless, skinless chicken breast halves (about 1 pound), cut into ½-inch strips
1 small red onion, sliced
1 (10-ounce) package frozen green peas, thawed, drained
1 yellow or red pepper, cut into strips
½ cup chicken broth
1 (8-ounce) container soft cream cheese with garlic and herb
Salt and black pepper

1. Cook pasta in lightly salted boiling water according to package directions (about 5 minutes); drain.

2. Meanwhile, heat oil in large skillet or wok over medium-high heat. Add chicken and onion; stir-fry 3 minutes or until chicken is no longer pink in center.

3. Add peas and yellow pepper; stir-fry 4 minutes. Reduce heat to medium.

4. Stir in broth and cream cheese. Cook, stirring constantly, until cream cheese is melted.

5. Combine pasta and chicken mixture in serving bowl; mix lightly. Season with salt and black pepper to taste. Garnish as desired.

Makes 4 servings

▲ Substitute dried bow tie pasta or fusilli for fresh pasta.

Today's supermarkets offer many brands and varieties of fresh pasta. You can usually find fresh pasta in the deli section or refrigerator case.

A faster cooking time makes fresh pasta more convenient than dried; fresh pasta usually cooks in 5 minutes or less, depending on desired doneness, while dried pasta requires 7 to 12 minutes cooking time. When substituting dried pasta for fresh, make sure to allow extra cooking time in your game plan.

Top left to bottom right: Tomatoes Vinaigrette (page 14), Creamy Herbed Chicken

Today, you can purchase a wide variety of fresh herbs from your local supermarket. While fresh herbs cost more than dried herbs, keep in mind that the improvement in flavor will be worth it.

Tomatoes Vinaigrette

2 large tomatoes, thinly sliced
3 tablespoons olive oil
1 tablespoon white wine vinegar
1 teaspoon sugar
1 teaspoon dried basil leaves, crushed, or 1 tablespoon fresh basil leaves
2 green onions, finely chopped
Salt and pepper

1. Arrange tomatoes on serving plate; set aside.

2. Whisk together oil, vinegar, sugar and basil. Stir in onions. Season with salt and pepper to taste.

3. When ready to serve, pour dressing over tomatoes.

Makes 4 servings

Strawberry Dessert Loaf

¾ cup whipping cream
2 tablespoons powdered sugar
1 teaspoon vanilla
½ cup strawberry slices
1 angel food cake loaf, cut lengthwise into 4 slices

1. Beat whipping cream at high speed with electric mixer until soft peaks form. Add powdered sugar and vanilla. Beat at high speed until stiff peaks form. Reserve half of the whipped cream; set aside. Fold strawberries into remaining whipped cream.

2. Place one cake slice on serving plate; spread with one third of the strawberry mixture. Repeat layers twice. Top with the remaining cake slice.

3. Frost with the reserved whipped cream. Refrigerate.

4. Slice loaf just before serving. Refrigerate leftovers.

Makes 4 to 6 servings

Soft Turkey Tacos

Cheesy Refried Beans

Creamy Citrus Pie

GAME PLAN

▲ **Prepare Creamy Citrus Pie (page 17).**

▲ **Warm tortillas.**

▲ **Chop onion for tacos and cook taco filling.**

▲ **While taco filling is cooking, heat beans and salsa for Cheesy Refried Beans (page 17).**

▲ **While taco filling and beans are cooking, chop tomatoes and shred lettuce for tacos.**

▲ **Assemble Soft Turkey Tacos and finish beans.**

Soft Turkey Tacos

8 (6-inch) corn tortillas
1½ teaspoons vegetable oil
1 pound ground turkey
1 small onion, chopped
1 teaspoon dried oregano leaves, crushed
Salt and pepper
Chopped tomatoes
Shredded lettuce
Salsa

1. Wrap tortillas in foil. Place in cold oven; set temperature to 350°F.

2. Heat oil in large skillet over medium heat. Add turkey and onion; cook until turkey is no longer pink, stirring occasionally. Stir in oregano. Season with salt and pepper to taste. Keep warm.

3. For each taco, fill tortilla with turkey mixture; top with tomatoes, lettuce and salsa.

Makes 4 servings

▲ Substitute eight (10-inch) flour tortillas for corn tortillas.

To warm tortillas in the microwave oven: Wrap tortillas loosely in damp paper towel. Microwave on HIGH 2 minutes or until hot.

Ground turkey's low fat content and excellent flavor make it a popular replacement for ground beef in a wide variety of recipes. Check your supermarket's poultry case for ground turkey as well as for other healthful alternatives, such as turkey sausage and turkey cutlets.

Cheesy Refried Beans

1 (30-ounce) can
    refried beans
½ cup salsa
½ cup (2 ounces)
    shredded
    Cheddar cheese
½ cup (2 ounces)
    shredded
    Monterey Jack
    cheese

1. Combine beans and salsa in medium saucepan. Cook over medium heat, stirring occasionally, until hot and bubbly.
2. Spoon into serving bowl; sprinkle with cheeses.
    Makes 4 servings

Cover and refrigerate any leftover Cheesy Refried Beans. Reheat and serve with tortilla chips as an impromptu bean dip.

Creamy Citrus Pie

2 (8-ounce) packages
    cream cheese,
    softened
1 (6-ounce) can
    frozen limeade
    concentrate,
    partially thawed
3 tablespoons sugar
2 teaspoons grated
    lime peel
    (optional)
1 (8-inch) graham
    cracker crumb
    crust
2 or 3 oranges,
    sectioned

1. Beat together cream cheese and limeade concentrate in medium bowl until smooth. Beat in sugar and lime peel.
2. Pour into pie crust; cover. Refrigerate 30 minutes or until chilled.
3. Top with oranges just before serving. Refrigerate leftovers.
    Makes 8 servings

▲ Substitute one (11-ounce) can mandarin orange sections, drained, for fresh orange sections.

Berry Citrus Pie:
Omit orange sections. Serve with strawberry sauce from Fruit Medley (page 40).

To soften cream cheese quickly, remove from packages and place in medium microwave-safe bowl. Microwave on MEDIUM (50%) 1½ to 2 minutes or until slightly softened, turning bowl after 1 minute.

For ease in serving crumb crust pie, dip pie plate just to rim in hot water 30 seconds to soften crust slightly. Cut and serve.

Top to bottom: Cheesy Refried Beans, Soft Turkey Tacos (page 15)

Turkey Cordon Bleu

Calico Vegetable Sauté

Peachy Strawberry Shortcake

GAME PLAN

▲ **Whip cream and combine fruit for dessert.**

▲ **Cut zucchini and cherry tomatoes.**

▲ **Prepare Turkey Cordon Bleu.**

▲ **While turkey is cooking, cook Calico Vegetable Sauté.**

▲ **Just before serving, assemble Peachy Strawberry Shortcake.**

Clockwise from top left: Peachy Strawberry Shortcake, Turkey Cordon Bleu, Calico Vegetable Sauté

Turkey Cordon Bleu

4 turkey cutlets
½ teaspoon dried oregano leaves, crushed
1 tablespoon oil
1 tablespoon butter
4 ham slices
4 Provolone cheese slices

1. Place turkey between sheets of plastic wrap; pound to ¼-inch thickness. Remove plastic wrap. Sprinkle turkey with oregano.

2. Heat oil and butter in large skillet over medium heat.

3. Add turkey; cook 8 minutes or until no longer pink in center, turning after 4 minutes. Season with pepper to taste, if desired.

4. Top each cutlet with ham and cheese; cover. Continue cooking 3 to 5 minutes or until cheese is melted. Garnish as desired.

Makes 4 servings

Calico Vegetable Sauté

1 tablespoon vegetable oil
2 medium zucchini, halved lengthwise, sliced crosswise
1 pint cherry tomatoes, halved
1 teaspoon dried basil leaves, crushed
Salt and pepper

1. Heat oil in medium skillet over medium heat; add zucchini. Cook 3 minutes, stirring occasionally.

2. Add tomatoes and basil. Season with salt and pepper to taste. Continue cooking 2 minutes or until thoroughly heated, stirring occasionally.

Makes 4 servings

Peachy Strawberry Shortcake

1 (10-ounce) package frozen strawberries with sugar, thawed
1 (8- to 10-ounce) package frozen peach slices, thawed
½ pint (1 cup) whipping cream
1 (9-inch) yellow cake layer

1. Drain strawberries, reserving juice. Combine strawberries and peaches; cover. Refrigerate.

2. Beat whipping cream at high speed with electric mixer until stiff peaks form; cover. Refrigerate.

3. When ready to serve, cut cake into wedges; drizzle with small amount of reserved strawberry juice. Top with fruit mixture and whipped cream. Refrigerate leftovers.

Makes 4 to 6 servings

Mini Turkey Loaves

Vegetable Stir-Fry

Creamy Mashed Potatoes

Apple pie

GAME PLAN

▲ **Preheat oven to 425°F.**

▲ **Boil water for potatoes.**

▲ **Prepare Mini Turkey Loaves.**

▲ **While turkey is baking, slice vegetables for stir-fry. Peel and cut potatoes.**

▲ **Cook potatoes.**

▲ **While potatoes are cooking, finish Vegetable Stir-Fry.**

▲ **Finish Creamy Mashed Potatoes.**

Mini Turkey Loaves

1 pound ground turkey
1 small apple, chopped
½ small onion, chopped
½ cup uncooked rolled oats
2 teaspoons Dijon-style mustard
1 teaspoon dried rosemary leaves, crushed
1 teaspoon salt
Dash of pepper

1. Preheat oven to 425°F. Grease twelve muffin cups.
2. Combine all ingredients. Press into prepared muffin cups.
3. Bake 20 minutes or until lightly browned and no longer pink in center. Garnish as desired. Serve with cranberry sauce, if desired.
Makes 4 servings

Vegetable Stir-Fry

1 tablespoon vegetable oil
3 or 4 carrots, diagonally sliced
2 zucchini, diagonally sliced
3 tablespoons orange juice
Salt and pepper

1. Heat oil in medium skillet or wok over medium heat. Add carrots; stir-fry 3 minutes.
2. Add zucchini and orange juice; stir-fry 4 minutes or until vegetables are crisp-tender. Season with salt and pepper to taste.
Makes 4 servings

Creamy Mashed Potatoes

2 pounds potatoes, peeled, cut into 1-inch pieces
Salt
2 tablespoons butter or margarine
⅓ to ½ cup milk
Dash of pepper
Dash of ground nutmeg

1. Cook potatoes in lightly salted boiling water 10 minutes or until tender; drain.
2. Add butter. Mash potatoes, adding enough milk for a good consistency. Season with pepper and nutmeg.
Makes 4 servings

Top to bottom: Creamy Mashed Potatoes, Mini Turkey Loaves with Vegetable Stir-Fry

Citrus Chicken

Poppy Seed Noodles

Garden Vegetable Medley

Blueberry pie

GAME PLAN

▲ **Boil water for noodles and for vegetables.**

▲ **Slice carrots.**

▲ **Cook chicken breasts.**

▲ **While chicken is cooking, mince garlic, section grapefruit and cook noodles, green beans and carrots.**

▲ **Finish Citrus Chicken, Poppy Seed Noodles and Garden Vegetable Medley.**

Clockwise on plate from top right: Citrus Chicken, Garden Vegetable Medley, Poppy Seed Noodles

Citrus Chicken

1 tablespoon
   vegetable oil
4 boneless, skinless
   chicken breast
   halves (about
   1 pound)
1 cup orange juice
4 teaspoons sugar
1 clove garlic, minced
1 teaspoon dried
   rosemary leaves,
   crushed
2 teaspoons
   cornstarch
¼ cup dry white wine
   Salt and pepper
2 pink grapefruit,
   sectioned

1. Heat oil in large skillet over medium heat. Add chicken; cook 8 minutes or until browned on both sides and no longer pink in center, turning after 4 minutes. Remove chicken from skillet; keep warm.

2. Add orange juice, sugar, garlic and rosemary to skillet; bring to a boil.

3. Combine cornstarch and wine. Add to skillet; cook, stirring constantly, until sauce is clear and thickened. Season with salt and pepper to taste.

4. Add grapefruit; heat thoroughly, stirring occasionally. Serve over chicken.
                    Makes 4 servings

Poppy Seed Noodles

8 ounces uncooked
   noodles
1 tablespoon butter or
   margarine
1 teaspoon poppy
   seeds

1. Cook noodles in lightly salted boiling water according to package directions; drain. Place in serving bowl.

2. Add butter and poppy seeds; toss lightly.
                    Makes 4 servings

Garden Vegetable Medley

1 pound fresh green
   beans
4 large carrots,
   diagonally sliced
2 tablespoons butter
   or margarine
¼ teaspoon dill weed
   (optional)
   Salt and pepper

1. Place 1 to 2 inches of water and steamer basket in large saucepan; bring water to a boil.

2. Add green beans and carrots; cover. Steam 10 minutes or until vegetables are crisp-tender.

3. Place vegetables in serving bowl. Add butter and dill weed; mix lightly. Season with salt and pepper to taste.
                    Makes 4 servings

Broiled Chicken Salad

Tortillas

Cherry Sundaes

GAME PLAN

▲ **Preheat broiler.**

▲ **Prepare Broiled Chicken Salad.**

▲ **Just before serving, prepare Cherry Sundaes.**

Broiled Chicken Salad

4 boneless, skinless chicken breast halves (about 1 pound)
1 (15-ounce) can black beans, drained, rinsed
2 green onions, chopped
  Bottled oil and vinegar dressing
1 (10-ounce) package frozen whole kernel corn, thawed, drained
2 tablespoons chopped pimento
2 tablespoons chopped cilantro
2 large tomatoes, cut into wedges

1. Preheat broiler. Position oven rack about 4 inches from heat source.
2. Place chicken on rack of broiler pan. Broil 8 minutes or until browned on both sides and no longer pink in center, turning after 4 minutes. Set aside.
3. Combine beans, onions and a small amount of dressing in medium bowl; mix lightly. Set aside.
4. Combine corn, pimento and chopped cilantro in separate bowl; mix lightly. Set aside.

5. Diagonally cut each chicken piece into thick slices; arrange on salad plates.
6. Arrange tomato wedges and spoonfuls of bean and corn mixtures around chicken. Garnish as desired.
7. Drizzle a small amount of dressing over chicken. Serve with additional dressing.
Makes 4 servings

Cherry Sundaes

1 quart ice cream, any flavor
1 cup cherry pie filling
¾ cup chocolate sauce, warmed

1. Scoop ice cream into individual dessert dishes.
2. Top with pie filling and chocolate sauce. Serve with cookies, if desired.
Makes 4 servings

To heat chocolate sauce in the microwave oven, pour sauce into 1-cup glass measuring cup. Microwave on HIGH 1 to 2 minutes or until thoroughly heated, stirring after each minute.

Top to bottom: Cherry Sundae, Broiled Chicken Salad

Chicken-Asparagus Salad

Sun-Dried Tomato Muffins

Glazed Orange Slices

GAME PLAN

▲ **Preheat oven to 425°F.**

▲ **Peel and slice oranges for Glazed Orange Slices (page 28).**

▲ **Prepare Sun-Dried Tomato Muffins (page 28).**

▲ **While muffins are baking, prepare Chicken-Asparagus Salad.**

▲ **Just before serving, finish dessert.**

Chicken-Asparagus Salad

1 (14½-ounce) can chicken broth
1 bay leaf
1 green onion, cut into 1-inch pieces
1 (¼-inch-thick) slice fresh ginger
4 boneless, skinless chicken breast halves (about 1 pound)
Mustard Vinaigrette (recipe follows)
½ pound asparagus spears, cut in half, cooked until crisp-tender
1 (8¾-ounce) can whole baby sweet corn, drained, rinsed
Spinach or lettuce leaves
3 small tomatoes, chopped

1. Combine broth, bay leaf, onion and ginger in medium saucepan. Bring to a boil.
2. Add chicken; reduce heat to low. Cover; simmer 8 minutes or until chicken is no longer pink in center. Remove from broth; cool slightly. (Reserve broth for another use, if desired.)
3. Meanwhile, prepare Mustard Vinaigrette.
4. Cut chicken diagonally into narrow strips; place in medium bowl with asparagus and corn. Add vinaigrette; toss lightly. Let marinate at room temperature 15 minutes. Drain, reserving vinaigrette.
5. Arrange chicken, asparagus and corn on individual spinach-lined salad plates. Top with tomatoes. Serve with reserved vinaigrette.
Makes 4 servings

Mustard Vinaigrette

2 tablespoons country-style Dijon mustard
½ cup seasoned rice vinegar
¼ cup vegetable oil
½ teaspoon sesame oil
Dash of pepper

Whisk together all ingredients.

You can find rice vinegar in Asian markets or in the Oriental food section of larger supermarkets. Slightly milder in flavor than most common vinegars, rice vinegar comes in both Chinese and Japanese varieties.

Clockwise from top left: Glazed Orange Slices (page 28), Sun-Dried Tomato Muffins (page 28), Chicken-Asparagus Salad

Sun-dried tomatoes are tomatoes that have been naturally or artificially dried. They retain an intense, sweet flavor when used in sauces, pizzas and other dishes calling for cooked tomatoes.

You can purchase sun-dried tomatoes either packed in oil in jars or packaged dry in cellophane. The oil-packed variety tends to be more expensive but benefits from being soaked in liquid, making them ready to use. The dry variety needs to be poached in liquid before being used (see package directions). Both varieties can be used either whole or chopped.

Sun-Dried Tomato Muffins

½ cup all-purpose flour
¼ cup whole-wheat flour
1 teaspoon baking powder
1 teaspoon sugar
¼ teaspoon pepper
⅛ teaspoon salt
½ cup milk
2 tablespoons vegetable oil
2 to 3 tablespoons chopped green olives
1 tablespoon chopped sun-dried tomatoes

1. Preheat oven to 425°F. Grease twelve (1¼-inch) miniature muffin cups.
2. Combine dry ingredients in medium bowl.
3. Whisk together milk and oil. Add to dry ingredients, mixing just until moistened. Gently stir in olives and tomatoes. Spoon batter into prepared muffin cups.
4. Bake 15 minutes or until lightly browned.
Makes 12 miniature muffins

Note: Recipe may be doubled.

Glazed Orange Slices

2 or 3 large oranges, peeled and sliced crosswise
¼ to ⅓ cup orange marmalade
½ cup shredded coconut

1. Preheat broiler. Position oven rack about 4 inches from heat source.
2. Arrange orange slices on rack of broiler pan. Spoon about ½ teaspoon orange marmalade over each slice.
3. Broil until glaze starts to bubble, about 2 minutes.
4. Top with coconut; broil 2 minutes or until lightly toasted.
Makes 4 servings

▲ Substitute apricot or strawberry preserves for orange marmalade.

Meat in Minutes

Beef and pork continue to be mainstays in the American diet. Who can resist Warm Steak Salad with Mustard Dressing, Pork Chops with Glazed Apples or Oriental Beef Kabobs? Why wait? Serve one of these irresistible recipes tonight!

Oriental Beef Kabobs (page 36)

MEAT - MENUS

Roast Beef in Onion Rolls
Potato Salad Plus
Brownie S'Mores
(pages 30-31)
▲

Glazed Ham with Sweet Potatoes
Buttered Brussels Sprouts
Whole-wheat dinner rolls
Pumpkin pie
(pages 32-33)
▲

Pepper Steak Sandwiches
Garden Pasta Salad
Fruity Dessert Cups
(pages 34-35)
▲

Oriental Beef Kabobs
Green Rice
Pear Dessert Crisp
(pages 36-37)
▲

Lamb Meatball & Bean Soup
Pita bread
Mixed Greens with Herbed Vinaigrette
Fruit Medley
(pages 38-40)
▲

Chilled Cantaloupe Soup
Warm Steak Salad with Mustard Dressing
Herbed French Bread
Brownies
(pages 41-43)
▲

Pork Chops with Glazed Apples
Nutty Vegetable Duo
Whole-grain rolls
Raspberry sherbet with cookies
(pages 44-45)
▲

Beefy Rice Salad Sandwiches
Chocolate Pudding Parfaits
(pages 46-47)
▲

Steamed Brats
German Sauerkraut
Pumpernickel bread
Raspberry Fluff
(pages 48-49)
▲

Peachy Wine Coolers
No-Fuss Antipasto Salad
Cheesy Bacon Pizzas
Ice Cream Sandwiches
(pages 50-52)
▲

Bold titles indicate recipes included

Roast Beef in Onion Rolls

Potato Salad Plus

Brownie S'Mores

GAME PLAN

▲ **Prepare Potato Salad Plus.**

▲ **Prepare Roast Beef in Onion Rolls.**

▲ **Just before serving, prepare Brownie S'Mores.**

Roast Beef in Onion Rolls

Horseradish Sauce (recipe follows)
2 onion rolls, split
½ pound sliced roast beef
4 tomato slices
Watercress or lettuce leaves

1. Prepare Horseradish Sauce; spread on rolls.
2. Fill rolls with beef, tomatoes and watercress. Serve with dill pickles and olives, if desired.

Makes 2 sandwiches

Horseradish Sauce

2 tablespoons mayonnaise
2 tablespoons sour cream
1 to 2 teaspoons prepared horseradish
1 teaspoon Dijon-style mustard

Combine ingredients; mix until well blended.

Potato Salad Plus

½ pound deli creamy potato salad
1 small celery stalk, chopped
2 tablespoons chopped onion
2 tablespoons chopped red pepper (optional)
⅛ teaspoon black pepper

Combine all ingredients; mix lightly.

Makes 2 servings

Brownie S'Mores

2 (about 3-inch) unfrosted brownie squares
6 small chocolate-mint candies
⅓ to ½ cup marshmallow creme
Chopped nuts

1. Place brownies on microwave-safe plate. Arrange three candies on each brownie. Microwave on HIGH 10 to 15 seconds or just until chocolate candy begins to soften.
2. Top each brownie with marshmallow creme. Microwave on HIGH 10 to 15 seconds or just until marshmallow creme begins to soften. Sprinkle with nuts.

Makes 2 servings

▲ Substitute other flavors of chocolate candy for mint candies.

Clockwise from top right: Potato Salad Plus, Roast Beef in Onion Roll, Brownie S'Mores

Glazed Ham with Sweet Potatoes

Buttered Brussels Sprouts

Whole-wheat dinner rolls

Pumpkin pie

GAME PLAN

▲ **Preheat broiler.**

▲ **Boil water for Brussels sprouts.**

▲ **Trim Brussels sprouts; cook.**

▲ **While Brussels sprouts are cooking, prepare Glazed Ham with Sweet Potatoes.**

▲ **Finish Buttered Brussels Sprouts.**

Glazed Ham with Sweet Potatoes

1 (1¼-pound) slice ham steak
1 (16-ounce) can sliced peaches, drained
1 (16-ounce) can sweet potatoes, drained
Maple syrup
2 tablespoons apricot jam or preserves
1 teaspoon Dijon-style mustard

1. Preheat broiler. Position oven rack about 4 inches from heat source.

2. Place ham in shallow pan. Surround with peaches and sweet potatoes; drizzle peaches and sweet potatoes with small amount of maple syrup.

3. Broil 5 minutes or until lightly browned.

4. Meanwhile, heat combined jam and mustard in microwave or in saucepan on rangetop until jam is melted; stir until well blended.

5. Turn ham, peaches and sweet potatoes over; brush ham with jam mixture. Drizzle peaches and sweet potatoes with additional maple syrup. Continue broiling 5 minutes or until thoroughly heated.
    Makes 4 servings

Buttered Brussels Sprouts

1 pound Brussels sprouts
2 tablespoons butter or margarine

1. Trim ends of Brussels sprouts.

2. Bring about 2 inches of lightly salted water to a boil in medium saucepan.

3. Add Brussels sprouts; return to a boil. Reduce heat; cover. Simmer 10 minutes or until crisp-tender; drain.

4. Spoon Brussel sprouts into serving bowl. Add butter; toss lightly to coat.   *Makes 4 servings*

If fresh Brussels sprouts are not available, substitute 4 cups thawed frozen Brussels sprouts for the fresh. Refer to package directions for suggested cooking time.

Top to bottom: Buttered Brussels Sprouts, Glazed Ham with Sweet Potatoes

Pepper Steak Sandwiches

Garden Pasta Salad

Fruity Dessert Cups

GAME PLAN

▲ **Prepare fruit mixture for Fruity Dessert Cups.**

▲ **Boil water for pasta; cut vegetables for pasta salad and for sandwiches.**

▲ **Cook pasta.**

▲ **While pasta is cooking, finish Pepper Steak Sandwiches.**

▲ **While steak is cooking, finish Garden Pasta Salad.**

▲ **Just before serving, finish dessert.**

Clockwise from top right: Fruity Dessert Cup, Garden Pasta Salad, Pepper Steak Sandwich

Pepper Steak Sandwiches

1½ teaspoons oil
 1 pound sirloin steak
 ½ teaspoon dried oregano leaves, crushed
 1 large onion, thinly sliced
 1 clove garlic, minced
 1 green pepper, cut into strips
 1 red pepper, cut into strips
   Salt and black pepper
 4 (6-inch) French bread rolls, split
 ½ cup (2 ounces) shredded Monterey Jack cheese

1. Heat oil in large nonstick skillet over medium-high heat. Add steak. Sprinkle with oregano. Cook 3 to 4 minutes or until steak is browned on both sides, turning after 2 minutes.

2. Add onion and garlic to steak in skillet. Continue cooking 3 minutes.

3. Add green and red peppers; cook until peppers are tender and steak is medium-rare, stirring occasionally.

4. Remove steak from skillet; slice thinly. Season with salt and black pepper to taste.

5. Return steak slices to skillet; mix lightly with vegetables. Fill rolls with steak mixture and cheese.
Makes 4 sandwiches

Garden Pasta Salad

1 (9-ounce) package fresh tri-color rotini or shell macaroni
 1 pint cherry tomatoes, halved
 1 zucchini, chopped
 ¼ to ⅓ cup bottled Italian dressing
 ¼ cup chopped fresh parsley
 ⅛ teaspoon pepper

1. Cook pasta in lightly salted boiling water according to package directions; drain.

2. Place pasta, tomatoes and zucchini in serving bowl.

3. Add enough dressing to moisten; toss lightly. Add parsley and pepper; toss lightly. Serve warm.
Makes 4 servings

Fruity Dessert Cups

1 (8-ounce) can pineapple chunks, drained
1¼ cups red grapes
 2 kiwifruit, peeled, sliced
 4 scoops vanilla ice cream
 ¼ cup orange-flavored liqueur (optional)

1. Combine fruits; cover. Refrigerate.

2. When ready to serve, spoon fruit mixture into individual dessert dishes. Top with ice cream; drizzle with liqueur.
Makes 4 servings

Oriental Beef Kabobs

Green Rice

Pear Dessert Crisp

GAME PLAN

▲ **Preheat broiler.**

▲ **Prepare Green Rice.**

▲ **While rice is cooking, prepare Oriental Beef Kabobs.**

▲ **While kabobs are broiling, prepare and assemble dessert.**

▲ **When kabobs are done, finish Pear Dessert Crisp.**

Oriental Beef Kabobs

1 tablespoon olive oil
1 tablespoon soy sauce
1 tablespoon seasoned rice vinegar
4 purchased beef kabobs

1. Preheat broiler. Position oven rack about 4 inches from heat source.
2. Whisk together oil, soy sauce and vinegar; brush on kabobs.
3. Arrange kabobs on rack of broiler pan. Broil 10 minutes or to desired doneness, turning after 5 minutes.

Makes 4 servings

Green Rice

2 cups chicken broth
1 cup uncooked rice
¼ cup chopped fresh parsley
¼ cup chopped green onions with tops
1 tablespoon butter or margarine

1. Combine broth and rice in medium saucepan. Bring to a boil; stir.

To chop fresh parsley the no-mess way, place parsley sprigs in 1-cup measuring cup; snip with kitchen scissors until finely chopped.

2. Reduce heat to low; cover. Simmer, without stirring, 15 minutes or until rice is tender and liquid is absorbed. *(Do not remove lid during cooking.)*
3. Remove saucepan from heat; stir in parsley, onions and butter. Cover; keep warm until ready to serve.   *Makes 4 servings*

Pear Dessert Crisp

1 (29-ounce) can pear halves, drained
½ cup uncooked rolled oats
2 tablespoons sugar
2 tablespoons cold butter or margarine, cut into pieces

1. Preheat broiler.
2. Arrange pears, cut side up, in 9-inch baking dish.
3. Combine oats and sugar. Cut in butter until mixture resembles coarse crumbs. Spoon about 1 tablespoon oat mixture into each pear half.
4. Broil 1½ minutes or until topping begins to brown. **(Caution: Topping browns quickly.)** Refrigerate leftovers.

Makes 6 servings

Oriental Beef Kabobs with Green Rice

Lamb Meatball & Bean Soup

Pita bread

Mixed Greens with Herbed Vinaigrette

Fruit Medley

GAME PLAN

▲ **Prepare strawberry sauce for Fruit Medley (page 40).**

▲ **Prepare Herbed Vinaigrette (page 40). Arrange greens and tomatoes for salad on salad plates; top with cheese.**

▲ **Prepare Lamb Meatball & Bean Soup.**

▲ **Just before serving, finish dessert.**

Top to bottom: Mixed Greens with Herbed Vinaigrette (page 40), Lamb Meatball & Bean Soup

Lamb Meatball & Bean Soup

1 pound ground lamb
¼ cup chopped onion
1 clove garlic, minced
1 teaspoon ground cumin
½ teaspoon salt
2 cups chicken broth
1 (10-ounce) package frozen chopped broccoli
1 large tomato, chopped
1 (15-ounce) can garbanzo beans or black-eyed peas, drained
½ teaspoon dried thyme leaves, crushed
Salt and pepper

1. Combine lamb, onion, garlic, cumin and salt; mix lightly. Shape into 1-inch balls.
2. Brown meatballs in large skillet over medium-high heat, turning occasionally.
3. Meanwhile, bring broth to a boil in large saucepan. Add broccoli and tomato; return to a boil. Reduce heat; cover.

4. When meatballs are browned, remove from skillet with slotted spoon. Add to broth with beans and thyme; simmer 5 minutes. Season with salt and pepper to taste.
Makes 4 to 6 servings

▲ Substitute 1½ cups fresh broccoli flowerets for 10-ounce package frozen chopped broccoli.

To quickly shape uniform meatballs, place meat mixture on cutting board; pat evenly into large square, one inch thick. With sharp knife, cut meat into 1-inch squares; shape each square into a ball.

Take advantage of torn salad greens and cut-up raw vegetables from the supermarket salad bar or produce section. These ready-to-use ingredients let you forego the washing and cleaning steps, making them a great timesaver in your game plan. Pick and choose your greens and vegetables according to your whim!

Mixed Greens with Herbed Vinaigrette

Herbed Vinaigrette (recipe follows)
6 to 8 cups torn mixed greens
1 pint yellow pear or cherry tomatoes
½ to ¾ cup crumbled blue cheese

1. Prepare Herbed Vinaigrette; set aside.
2. Arrange greens and tomatoes on individual salad plates; sprinkle with blue cheese. Serve with vinaigrette.

Makes 4 to 6 servings

Herbed Vinaigrette

½ cup vegetable oil
2 tablespoons white wine vinegar
2 tablespoons seasoned rice vinegar
1 tablespoon chopped fresh parsley
1 tablespoon snipped fresh chives
Salt and pepper

Whisk together oil and vinegars. Whisk in parsley and chives. Season with salt and pepper to taste.

Fruit Medley

1 (10-ounce) package frozen strawberries with sugar, thawed
2 to 3 large bananas

1. Place strawberries in food processor or blender container; process until smooth. Cover; refrigerate.
2. When ready to serve, slice bananas into individual dessert dishes. Top with strawberry sauce.

Makes 4 to 6 servings

Use Fruit Medley as a topping for ice cream.

Chilled Cantaloupe Soup

Warm Steak Salad with Mustard Dressing

Herbed French Bread

Brownies

GAME PLAN

▲ **Prepare Chilled Cantaloupe Soup.**

▲ **Preheat broiler.**

▲ **Prepare Warm Steak Salad with Mustard Dressing.**

▲ **While steak is broiling, slice bread for Herbed French Bread (page 43). Prepare Herb Butter and spread on bread.**

▲ **When steak is done, broil bread.**

▲ **Arrange salad on platter.**

Chilled Cantaloupe Soup

½ medium to large
    cantaloupe, rind
    removed, seeded,
    cut into cubes
¼ cup plain yogurt
¾ cup half-and-half
    Salt and white
    pepper

1. Place cantaloupe in food processor or blender container; process until smooth.

2. Add yogurt; process until blended.

3. Pour cantaloupe mixture into medium bowl; stir in half-and-half. Season with salt and pepper to taste; cover. Refrigerate until ready to serve. Garnish as desired.

Makes 4 servings

▲ Substitute sour cream for plain yogurt.

Summer Honeydew Soup:
Substitute ½ medium honeydew melon for cantaloupe.

Cool Cucumber Soup:
Substitute one large or two medium seeded, peeled cucumbers for cantaloupe.

Warm Steak Salad with Mustard Dressing

Mustard Dressing
    (page 43)
1 beef flank steak
    (about
    1¼ pounds)
Salt and pepper
¼ pound sugar snap
    peas or snow peas
    Lettuce leaves
1 medium red onion,
    sliced, separated
    into rings
1 pint cherry
    tomatoes

1. Preheat broiler. Position oven rack about 4 inches from heat source.

2. Prepare Mustard Dressing; set aside.

3. Place steak on rack of broiler pan. Broil 10 minutes or to desired doneness, turning after 5 minutes. Season with salt and pepper to taste.

4. Meanwhile, bring lightly salted water to a boil in medium saucepan. Add peas; cook 2 minutes. Drain.

5. Place steak on cutting board. Cut diagonally across grain of meat into thin slices.

6. Line serving platter with lettuce. Arrange steak slices in center of platter. Surround with onion rings, snow peas and cherry tomatoes. Serve with dressing.

Makes 4 servings

Continued

Mustard Dressing

¾ cup olive oil
3 tablespoons
    seasoned rice
    vinegar
1 tablespoon balsamic
    vinegar
1 tablespoon
    Dijon-style
    mustard
¼ teaspoon dried
    thyme leaves,
    crushed
Salt and pepper

Whisk together oil,
vinegars, mustard and
thyme. Season with salt
and pepper to taste.

▲ Substitute coarse-
grind mustard for Dijon-
style mustard.

Balsamic vinegar is
a special aged
vinegar. Use in
small amounts to
add flavor to salads
and cooked dishes.

Herbed French Bread

Herb Butter
    (recipe follows)
1 French bread loaf,
    sliced

1. Preheat broiler.
2. Prepare Herb Butter.
3. Spread bread with
butter mixture.
(Refrigerate any leftover
Herb Butter.) Place bread
slices, spread side up, on
baking sheet.
4. Broil until butter
mixture is bubbly and
bread is lightly toasted.
Serve warm.
            Makes 4 servings

Herb Butter

½ cup butter or
    margarine,
    softened
2 tablespoons
    chopped fresh
    parsley
1 clove garlic, minced
1 tablespoon snipped
    fresh chives
1 tablespoon grated
    Parmesan cheese

Combine all ingredients;
mix until well blended.

Cut leftover Herbed
French Bread into
cubes for tasty
croutons. Just add to
your favorite tossed
green salad for a zesty
crunch or freeze in
freezer-weight plastic
bags for later use.

*Top to bottom: Chilled
Cantaloupe Soup (page
41), Warm Steak Salad
with Mustard Dressing
(page 41)*

Pork Chops with Glazed Apples

Nutty Vegetable Duo

Whole-grain rolls

Raspberry sherbet with cookies

GAME PLAN

▲ **Prepare Pork Chops with Glazed Apples.**

▲ **While pork chops are cooking, prepare Nutty Vegetable Duo.**

Pork Chops with Glazed Apples

1 tablespoon vegetable oil
4 boneless pork chops, 1/4 inch thick
1/2 teaspoon ground sage
Salt and pepper
2 large Granny Smith apples, thinly sliced
2 tablespoons sugar
1/2 teaspoon ground cinnamon

1. Heat oil in large skillet over medium heat. Add pork chops; sprinkle with sage.

2. Cook 8 minutes or until no longer pink in center, turning after 4 minutes. Season with salt and pepper to taste. Remove pork chops from skillet; keep warm.

3. Add apples, sugar and cinnamon to skillet. Reduce heat to low; cover. Cook 5 minutes, stirring occasionally. Serve over pork chops.
Makes 4 servings

Nutty Vegetable Duo

1 (10-ounce) package frozen green beans
1/2 (16-ounce) package frozen small whole onions
1/4 cup toasted slivered almonds
2 tablespoons butter or margarine
Salt and pepper

1. Combine beans and onions in medium saucepan; cook according to package directions. Drain.

2. Return vegetables to saucepan. Add almonds and butter; stir over low heat until butter is melted and mixture is thoroughly heated. Season with salt and pepper to taste.
Makes 4 servings

To toast almonds, spread almonds evenly in shallow baking pan. Bake at 350°F, 8 to 10 minutes or until lightly toasted, stirring occasionally.

Left to right on plate: Pork Chops with Glazed Apples, Nutty Vegetable Duo

Beefy Rice Salad Sandwiches

Chocolate Pudding Parfaits

GAME PLAN

▲ **Prepare Chocolate Pudding Parfaits.**

▲ **Prepare Beefy Rice Salad Sandwiches.**

Beefy Rice Salad Sandwiches

¾ pound lean ground beef
½ small onion, chopped
½ teaspoon dried thyme leaves, crushed
1½ cups cooked rice
½ red pepper, chopped
½ avocado, peeled, pitted and chopped
¼ cup chopped fresh parsley
3 tablespoons olive oil
3 tablespoons seasoned rice vinegar
Salt and black pepper
3 pita bread rounds, cut in half
Lettuce leaves
Tomato slices

1. Brown meat with onion over medium-high heat. Stir in thyme.

2. Combine rice, red pepper, avocado and parsley in medium bowl. Add meat mixture; mix lightly.

3. Whisk together oil and vinegar. Pour over meat mixture; toss lightly. Season with salt and black pepper to taste.

4. Fill pita halves with lettuce, tomatoes and meat mixture.

Makes 6 sandwiches

Chocolate Pudding Parfaits

2 ounces semisweet chocolate, chopped
2 ounces white chocolate, chopped
½ cup sugar
2 tablespoons flour
1 tablespoon cornstarch
2¼ cups milk
2 egg yolks, beaten
2 teaspoons vanilla, divided

1. Place semisweet chocolate and white chocolate in separate heatproof bowls; set aside.

2. Combine sugar, flour and cornstarch in saucepan. Gradually whisk in milk. Cook, stirring constantly, over medium heat until mixture comes to a boil. Boil 2 minutes, stirring constantly.

3. Remove saucepan from heat. Stir small amount of hot mixture into beaten egg yolks; return to hot mixture in pan. Cook and stir until thickened.

4. Spoon half of the egg mixture over each of the two chocolates in bowls; stir until chocolates are completely melted. Blend 1 teaspoon vanilla into each bowl.

5. Alternate layers of puddings in parfait glasses; cover. Refrigerate.

Makes 3 to 4 servings

Top to bottom: Chocolate Pudding Parfait, Beefy Rice Salad Sandwiches

Steamed Brats

German Sauerkraut

Pumpernickel bread

Raspberry Fluff

GAME PLAN

▲ **Tear cake into pieces and whip cream for dessert.**

▲ **Prepare German Sauerkraut.**

▲ **While sauerkraut is cooking, prepare Steamed Brats.**

▲ **Just before serving, assemble Raspberry Fluff.**

Steamed Brats

8 fully cooked bratwurst
½ cup beer or water

1. Pierce bratwurst with fork.

2. Place bratwurst and beer in medium skillet. Bring to a boil. Reduce heat to medium; cover. Simmer 5 minutes.

3. Remove lid; continue simmering until beer is evaporated. Cook until bratwurst are browned, turning occasionally. Serve with mustard, if desired.

Makes 4 servings

German Sauerkraut

1 (32-ounce) jar sauerkraut, drained
2 Golden Delicious apples, quartered, sliced
1 cup apple juice
1 bay leaf
8 juniper berries (optional)

1. Combine all ingredients in large saucepan. Bring to a boil.

2. Reduce heat to medium. Simmer 15 minutes or until apples are tender and liquid is almost evaporated, stirring occasionally.

3. Remove bay leaf and juniper berries before serving.

Makes 4 servings

Raspberry Fluff

½ angel food cake loaf
½ pint (1 cup) whipping cream
1 (10-ounce) package frozen raspberries, thawed, drained

1. Tear cake into small pieces; cover. Set aside.

2. Beat whipping cream at high speed with electric mixer until stiff peaks form; cover. Refrigerate.

3. When ready to serve, combine cake and raspberries in medium bowl; mix lightly. Fold in whipped cream. Spoon into individual dessert dishes. Garnish as desired. Refrigerate leftovers.

Makes 4 to 6 servings

▲ Substitute 1½ to 2 cups fresh raspberries for frozen raspberries.

Left to right on plate:
Steamed Brats,
German Sauerkraut

Peachy Wine Coolers

No-Fuss Antipasto Salad

Cheesy Bacon Pizzas

Ice Cream Sandwiches

GAME PLAN

▲ **Preheat oven to 450°F.**

▲ **Prepare Ice Cream Sandwiches (page 52).**

▲ **Prepare Cheesy Bacon Pizzas (page 52).**

▲ **While pizzas are baking, prepare No-Fuss Antipasto Salad.**

▲ **Just before serving, prepare Peachy Wine Coolers.**

Clockwise from top left: Peachy Wine Cooler, Ice Cream Sandwiches (page 52), No-Fuss Antipasto Salad, Cheesy Bacon Pizza (page 52)

Peachy Wine Coolers

1 cup dry white wine
½ cup peach or apricot nectar
1 cup carbonated mineral water
Ice cubes

1. Combine wine, nectar and water in small pitcher.
2. Add ice to two tall glasses.
3. Fill glasses with wine mixture. Garnish as desired.
Makes 2 servings

No-Fuss Antipasto Salad

1 (6-ounce) jar marinated artichoke hearts, undrained
½ teaspoon white wine vinegar
1 teaspoon snipped fresh chives
¼ teaspoon dried oregano leaves, crushed
¼ teaspoon dried basil leaves, crushed
⅛ teaspoon pepper
8 cherry tomatoes, halved
10 pitted ripe olives, halved

1. Drain artichoke hearts, reserving liquid. Add vinegar, chives, oregano, basil and pepper to liquid to make dressing.
2. Pour dressing over combined tomatoes and olives; toss lightly.
3. Arrange tomato mixture and artichokes on serving platter.
Makes 2 servings

▲ Substitute ½ (14-ounce) can plain artichoke hearts, drained and quartered, for 6-ounce jar marinated artichoke hearts, and substitute 2 tablespoons olive oil for the drained artichoke marinade.

Have an herb garden? Substitute fresh herbs for dried herbs in any of these recipes; just use three times the dried amount. For example, in this tasty antipasto salad you would increase measurements of dried oregano and basil to ¾ teaspoon fresh herbs each.

Italian bread shells, a relatively new addition to the supermarket shelves, can usually be found in either the deli or fresh food sections of larger supermarkets. These shelf-stable shells, deliciously seasoned with Italian cheeses and herbs, give you a "homemade" pizza crust with a pizzeria taste.

Cheesy Bacon Pizzas

2 (8-inch) Italian bread shells
6 to 8 tomato slices
1/4 teaspoon dried basil leaves, crushed
1/4 teaspoon dried oregano leaves, crushed
Dash of pepper
3 ounces Canadian bacon, chopped
3/4 cup (3 ounces) shredded Monterey Jack cheese

1. Preheat oven to 450°F.
2. Place bread shells on cookie sheet. Top with tomatoes. Sprinkle with basil, oregano and pepper. Top with bacon and cheese.
3. Bake 8 minutes or until cheese is melted.
Makes 2 servings

▲ Substitute pita bread rounds for Italian bread shells.

Ice Cream Sandwiches

4 large chocolate chip cookies
1 cup ice cream, slightly softened

1. For each sandwich, cover one cookie with 1/2 cup ice cream; top with second cookie.
2. Wrap cookie sandwiches individually in plastic wrap; freeze until ready to serve. If necessary, let stand at room temperature about 5 minutes before serving to soften slightly.
Makes 2 cookie sandwiches

Double this recipe to make extra Ice Cream Sandwiches to keep on hand for last-minute snacks.

Party Idea: To make sixteen Ice Cream Sandwiches, divide one (1-gallon) carton of ice cream, softened, into sixteen equal portions using a wet table knife. Assemble sandwiches as directed, working quickly. Wrap and freeze until ready to serve.

Simple Seafood

Experience exciting new alternatives to plain broiled fish with this unbeatable collection of creative seafood recipes—everything from Nutty Pan-Fried Trout to colorful Garlic Shrimp & Vegetables.

Nutty Pan-Fried Trout (page 64)

SEAFOOD - MENUS

Thai Tea
Scallop Stir-Fry
Tropical Fruit Compote
Fortune cookies
(pages 54-55)

▲

Vegetable-Shrimp
Stir-Fry
Oh-So-Easy Rice
Berried Cantaloupe
with Honey Dressing
(pages 56-57)

▲

Baked Halibut with
Roasted Pepper Sauce
Lemony Steamed
Broccoli
Oven-Baked Potatoes
Peach yogurt with
peach slices
(pages 58-59)

▲

Poached Salmon with
Basil Mayonnaise
Pea-Pod Medley
Couscous
Strawberries Elegante
(pages 60-61)

▲

Mediterranean
Tuna Salad
Bread sticks
Brownie Sundaes
(pages 62-63)

▲

Nutty Pan-Fried Trout
Tri-Color Pasta
Minty Peas
Ice Cream with
Gingered Apples
(pages 64-66)

▲

Broiled Orange Roughy
with
Green Peppercorn Sauce
Seasoned New Potatoes
Steamed Broccoli &
Carrots
Fruity Shortcake Slices
(pages 67-69)

▲

Oyster Poor Boys
Cole Slaw Vinaigrette
Orange slices with
vanilla yogurt
(pages 70-71)

▲

Salmon, Fettuccine
& Cabbage
Sourdough rolls
Make-It-Easy
Lemon Tarts
(pages 72-73)

▲

Garlic Shrimp &
Vegetables
Cheesy Lahvosh
Spinach Fettuccine
Honey-Glazed
Pineapple Slices
(pages 74-75)

▲

Savory Seafood Soup
French bread
Tossed Green Salad with
Buttermilk Dressing
Fruity Cookies & Cream
(pages 76-78)

▲

Bold titles indicate recipes included

Thai Tea

Scallop Stir-Fry

Tropical Fruit Compote

Fortune cookies

GAME PLAN

▲ Boil water for noodles and for tea.

▲ Cut vegetables and scallops for stir-fry.

▲ Steep tea.

▲ While tea is steeping, prepare fruit mixture for fruit compote.

▲ Remove tea bags; cool tea.

▲ While tea is cooling, finish Scallop Stir-Fry.

▲ Finish Thai Tea.

▲ Just before serving, finish Tropical Fruit Compote.

Thai Tea

4 tea bags
4 cups boiling water
½ cup sweetened condensed milk
Ice cubes

1. Place tea bags in teapot or other heatproof container. Add boiling water; steep 4 minutes. Remove tea bags. Cool tea slightly.
2. Spoon 2 tablespoons sweetened condensed milk into each of four tall glasses. Add ice cubes. Fill with tea. Stir to combine.
Makes 4 servings

Scallop Stir-Fry

6 ounces uncooked ramen noodles
1 tablespoon olive oil
1 pound asparagus, cut into 1-inch pieces
1 red pepper, cut into thin rings
3 green onions, chopped
1 large clove garlic, minced
1 pound sea scallops, halved crosswise
2 tablespoons soy sauce
1 teaspoon hot pepper sauce
1 teaspoon sesame oil
Juice of ½ lime

1. Cook noodles in lightly salted boiling water according to package directions.
2. Meanwhile, heat olive oil in wok or large skillet over high heat. Add asparagus, red pepper, onions and garlic. Stir-fry 2 minutes.
3. Add scallops; stir-fry until scallops turn opaque.
4. Stir in soy sauce, hot pepper sauce, sesame oil and lime juice. Add noodles; heat thoroughly, stirring occasionally.
Makes 4 servings

▲ Substitute vermicelli for ramen noodles.

Tropical Fruit Compote

1 banana
Lemon juice
2 kiwifruit, peeled, sliced
1 (8-ounce) can pineapple tidbits, drained
1 papaya, cut into chunks
Shredded coconut (optional)

1. Cut banana into chunks. Place in medium bowl; toss with enough lemon juice to coat to prevent browning.
2. Add kiwifruit, pineapple and papaya; mix lightly. Cover; refrigerate.
3. When ready to serve, spoon fruit mixture into individual dessert dishes; sprinkle with coconut.
Makes 4 servings

Vegetable-Shrimp Stir-Fry

Oh-So-Easy Rice

Berried Cantaloupe with Honey Dressing

GAME PLAN

▲ Prepare Oh-So-Easy Rice.

▲ While bringing broth to a boil, prepare Honey Dressing and cantaloupe shells.

▲ While rice is simmering, prepare Vegetable-Shrimp Stir-Fry.

▲ Just before serving, finish dessert.

Vegetable-Shrimp Stir-Fry

1 tablespoon olive oil
6 ounces snow peas, trimmed
6 green onions, cut into 1-inch pieces
1 red pepper, cut into ½-inch strips
1 pound peeled, deveined medium shrimp
¼ pound large mushrooms, quartered
2 tablespoons soy sauce
1 tablespoon seasoned rice vinegar
1 teaspoon sesame oil

1. Heat olive oil in large skillet or wok over medium-high heat. Add snow peas, onions and red pepper; stir-fry 2 minutes.

2. Add shrimp; stir-fry 2 minutes or until shrimp turn pink.

3. Add mushrooms; stir-fry until tender and most of liquid evaporates.

4. Add remaining ingredients; heat thoroughly, stirring constantly.
Makes 4 servings

Oh-So-Easy Rice

2 cups chicken broth
1 cup uncooked rice
1 tablespoon butter or margarine

1. Combine broth and rice in medium saucepan. Bring to a boil; stir.

2. Reduce heat to low; cover. Simmer 15 minutes or until rice is tender and liquid is absorbed. *(Do not remove lid during cooking.)*

3. Remove saucepan from heat; stir in butter. Cover; keep warm until ready to serve.
Makes 4 servings

Berried Cantaloupe with Honey Dressing

Honey Dressing (recipe follows)
2 small cantaloupes
2 cups raspberries

1. Prepare Honey Dressing; cover. Refrigerate.

2. Cut cantaloupes in half; remove seeds. Cover; refrigerate.

3. When ready to serve, place cantaloupe halves in individual bowls; fill centers with raspberries. Drizzle with dressing.
Makes 4 servings

Honey Dressing

1 cup plain yogurt
2 tablespoons honey
2 teaspoons grated orange peel

Combine all ingredients; mix until well blended.

Top to bottom: Berried Cantaloupe with Honey Dressing, Vegetable-Shrimp Stir-Fry with Oh-So-Easy Rice

*Baked Halibut
with Roasted
Pepper Sauce*

*Lemony Steamed
Broccoli*

*Oven-Baked
Potatoes*

*Peach yogurt with
peach slices*

GAME PLAN

▲ **Preheat oven to
425°F.**

▲ **Prepare Baked
Halibut with
Roasted Pepper
Sauce.**

▲ **Boil water for
broccoli.**

▲ **While fish is
baking, prepare
Oven-Baked
Potatoes. Bake
potatoes with fish
during last 10
minutes of fish
baking time.**

▲ **While potatoes
are baking,
prepare Lemony
Steamed
Broccoli.**

*Clockwise from top:
Lemony Steamed Broccoli,
Baked Halibut with
Roasted Pepper Sauce,
Oven-Baked Potatoes*

Baked Halibut
with Roasted
Pepper Sauce

Roasted Pepper
Sauce
(recipe follows)
1 medium onion,
thinly sliced
1 large clove garlic,
minced
1 (1½-pound) halibut
fillet, skinned

1. Preheat oven to 425°F.
Grease shallow baking
dish.
2. Prepare Roasted
Pepper Sauce; set aside.
3. Cover bottom of
prepared baking dish
with onion and garlic.
Top with fish and sauce.
4. Bake 20 minutes or
until fish flakes easily
when tested with fork.
Garnish as desired.
Makes 4 to 6 servings

Roasted Pepper Sauce

1 (7-ounce) can
chopped green
chilies, drained
1 (7-ounce) jar
roasted red
peppers, drained
⅔ cup chicken broth

Combine ingredients in
food processor or
blender container;
process until smooth.

Lemony Steamed
Broccoli

1 pound broccoli
1 tablespoon butter
2 teaspoons lemon
juice
Salt and pepper

1. Break broccoli into
flowerets. Discard large
stems. Trim smaller
stems; cut stems into thin
slices.
2. Place 2 to 3 inches of
water and steamer
basket in large saucepan;
bring water to a boil.
3. Add broccoli; cover.
Steam 6 minutes or until
crisp-tender.
4. Place broccoli in
serving bowl. Add butter
and lemon juice; toss
lightly to coat. Season
with salt and pepper to
taste. *Makes 4 servings*

Oven-Baked
Potatoes

2 large baking
potatoes (about
10 ounces each)
2 tablespoons butter
or margarine,
melted
2 tablespoons
vegetable oil
Salt and pepper

1. Preheat oven to 425°F.
2. Scrub potatoes; do not
peel. Thinly slice
potatoes crosswise. Pat
potato slices dry with
paper towels.
3. Place potatoes in
medium bowl. Add
butter and oil; toss
lightly to coat. Place on
nonstick baking sheet.
4. Bake 10 minutes or
until tender and lightly
browned, stirring lightly
after 5 minutes. Season
with salt and pepper to
taste. *Makes 4 servings*

Poached Salmon with Basil Mayonnaise

Pea-Pod Medley

Couscous

Strawberries Elegante

GAME PLAN

▲ **Prepare strawberry-sugar mixture for Strawberries Elegante.**

▲ **Cut vegetables for Basil Mayonnaise and for Pea-Pod Medley.**

▲ **Cook couscous.**

▲ **While couscous is cooking, finish Poached Salmon with Basil Mayonnaise.**

▲ **While salmon is cooking, finish Pea-Pod Medley.**

▲ **Just before serving, finish dessert.**

Poached Salmon with Basil Mayonnaise

Basil Mayonnaise (recipe follows)
1 bay leaf
4 peppercorns
4 salmon steaks, 1 to 1½ inches thick

1. Prepare Basil Mayonnaise; cover. Set aside.
2. Add bay leaf, peppercorns and enough water to medium skillet to fill to 1-inch depth. Bring to a boil. Add salmon.
3. Reduce heat; cover. Simmer 5 minutes or until salmon flakes easily when tested with fork.
4. Remove salmon from poaching liquid; serve with Basil Mayonnaise.
Makes 4 servings

Basil Mayonnaise
½ cup mayonnaise
½ cup sour cream or plain yogurt
1 green onion, cut into 1-inch pieces
2 tablespoons fresh parsley
2 tablespoons fresh basil
Salt and pepper

Combine mayonnaise, sour cream, onion, parsley and basil in food processor or blender container; process until well blended. Season with salt and pepper to taste.

Pea-Pod Medley

2 tablespoons oil
½ pound snow peas, trimmed
¼ pound mushrooms, sliced
1 yellow or red pepper, cut into strips
Salt and black pepper

1. Heat oil over medium-high heat in large skillet or wok. Add vegetables.
2. Stir-fry 4 minutes or until vegetables are crisp-tender. Season with salt and black pepper to taste.   *Makes 4 servings*

Strawberries Elegante

1 pint strawberries, halved
2 tablespoons sugar
6 tablespoons half-and-half
2 tablespoons orange-flavored liqueur
1 tablespoon anise-flavored liqueur
⅛ teaspoon pepper
4 scoops vanilla ice cream

1. Combine strawberries and sugar in medium bowl; cover. Refrigerate.
2. When ready to serve, stir half-and-half, liqueurs and pepper into strawberry mixture. Serve over ice cream.
Makes 4 servings

Left to right: Pea-Pod Medley, Poached Salmon with Basil Mayonnaise

Mediterranean Tuna Salad

Bread sticks

Brownie Sundaes

GAME PLAN

▲ **Prepare Mediterranean Tuna Salad.**

▲ **Just before serving, prepare Brownie Sundaes.**

Mediterranean Tuna Salad

¼ pound fresh green beans
1 (12-ounce) can tuna, drained, separated into chunks
2 tablespoons capers (optional)
1 (15-ounce) can Great Northern beans, drained, rinsed
1 large tomato, chopped
12 ripe Greek olives
Snipped fresh chives (optional)
Bottled Italian dressing

1. Cook green beans in lightly salted boiling water 5 minutes or until crisp-tender; drain. Rinse with cold water; drain again.
2. Place tuna in center of serving platter; sprinkle with capers.
3. Arrange beans, tomatoes and olives around tuna; surround with green beans. Sprinkle with chives, if desired. Serve with dressing.
Makes 4 servings

Brownie Sundaes

1 cup marshmallow creme
3 to 4 teaspoons milk
4 brownies
4 scoops ice cream, any flavor

1. Combine marshmallow creme and 3 teaspoons milk in small saucepan. Stir over medium-low heat until marshmallow creme is melted and mixture is smooth. (Add additional milk if necessary for good pouring consistency.) Keep warm.
2. Place brownies in individual dessert dishes. Top with ice cream and marshmallow sauce.
Makes 4 servings

If using a 7-ounce jar of marshmallow creme, mix one (3-ounce) package softened cream cheese with the remaining marshmallow creme for a quick fruit dip.

Nutty Pan-Fried Trout

Tri-Color Pasta

Minty Peas

Ice Cream with Gingered Apples

GAME PLAN

▲ **Boil water for Tri-Color Pasta and for Minty Peas (page 66).**

▲ **Chop mint for peas.**

▲ **Prepare and cook apple mixture for Ice Cream with Gingered Apples (page 66).**

▲ **While apples are cooking, prepare Nutty Pan-Fried Trout.**

▲ **While trout is cooking, finish Tri-Color Pasta and Minty Peas.**

▲ **Just before serving, finish dessert.**

Nutty Pan-Fried Trout

2 tablespoons oil
4 trout fillets (about 6 ounces each)
½ cup seasoned bread crumbs
½ cup pine nuts

1. Heat oil in large skillet over medium heat. Lightly coat fish with crumbs. Add to skillet.

2. Cook 8 minutes or until fish flakes easily when tested with fork, turning after 5 minutes. Remove fish from skillet. Place on serving platter; keep warm.

3. Add nuts to drippings in skillet. Cook and stir 3 minutes or until nuts are lightly toasted. Sprinkle over fish.

Makes 4 servings

Pine nuts are seeds which grow inside the cones of several varieties of pine trees. Purchase pine nuts in health food stores, nut shops or large supermarkets. Store pine nuts in a plastic bag or airtight container and refrigerate up to 3 months or freeze up to 9 months. For a tasty alternative, you may substitute slivered almonds for the pine nuts in this recipe.

Tri-Color Pasta

1 (9-ounce) package fresh tri-color pasta shells
¼ cup grated Parmesan cheese (optional)
1 tablespoon butter or margarine
¼ teaspoon dried basil leaves, crushed (optional)
Salt and pepper

1. Cook pasta in lightly salted boiling water according to package directions (about 5 minutes); drain. Place in medium serving bowl.

2. Add cheese, butter and basil leaves; toss lightly to coat. Season with salt and pepper to taste.

Makes 4 servings

▲ Substitute dried tri-color pasta shells for fresh pasta.

Clockwise from top: Minty Peas (page 66), Nutty Pan-Fried Trout, Tri-Color Pasta

When buying fresh ginger, select roots with smooth, unwrinkled skin. To use, peel the tough skin away to expose the tender root underneath; peel only as needed.

You can store *unpeeled* ginger tightly wrapped in the refrigerator for up to one week; unpeeled ginger can also be frozen, tightly wrapped, for up to two months.

To store *peeled* ginger, place in a tight-sealing jar and cover with dry sherry. Refrigerate for up to three weeks. You can use the ginger-flavored sherry in cooking as well.

Minty Peas

1 (10-ounce) package frozen green peas
1 tablespoon butter or margarine
1 tablespoon chopped fresh mint *or*
   1 teaspoon dried mint leaves
Salt and pepper

1. Cook peas according to package directions; drain. Place peas in serving bowl.
2. Add butter and mint; mix lightly to coat. Season with salt and pepper to taste.
Makes 4 servings

Cashew Pea Salad:
Omit butter, salt and pepper. Thaw peas and drain. *Do not cook.* Add ½ cup cashews with mint to peas.

Ice Cream with Gingered Apples

2 tablespoons butter or margarine
2 large or 4 small Golden Delicious apples, thinly sliced
2 tablespoons packed brown sugar
1 teaspoon minced fresh ginger *or* ¼ teaspoon ground ginger
4 scoops vanilla ice cream

1. Melt butter in medium saucepan over medium heat. Stir in apple slices, sugar and ginger.
2. Cook 6 minutes or until apples are tender and glazed, stirring occasionally. Serve over ice cream.
Makes 4 servings

Note: Apples may be made ahead and reheated just before serving, if desired.

Broiled Orange Roughy with Green Peppercorn Sauce

Seasoned New Potatoes

Steamed Broccoli & Carrots

Fruity Shortcake Slices

GAME PLAN

▲ **Preheat broiler.**

▲ **Boil water for potatoes and for Steamed Broccoli & Carrots (page 68).**

▲ **Prepare Broiled Orange Roughy with Green Peppercorn Sauce.**

▲ **While fish is broiling, cook potatoes and steam broccoli and carrots.**

▲ **While vegetables are cooking, prepare Yogurt Sauce for Fruity Shortcake Slices (page 68).**

▲ **After broiling fish, broil cake slices for dessert.**

▲ **Finish potatoes, broccoli and carrots.**

▲ **Just before serving, finish dessert.**

Broiled Orange Roughy with Green Peppercorn Sauce

Green Peppercorn Sauce (recipe follows)
4 orange roughy fillets (about 6 ounces each)

1. Preheat broiler. Position oven rack about 4 inches from heat source.
2. Prepare Green Peppercorn Sauce; set aside.
3. Place fish in shallow baking pan; top with sauce.
4. Broil 10 minutes or until fish flakes easily when tested with fork.

Makes 4 servings

Green Peppercorn Sauce

1 cup loosely packed cilantro leaves
2 tablespoons country-style Dijon mustard
2 tablespoons dry white wine
½ teaspoon green peppercorns, rinsed, drained

Combine ingredients in food processor or blender container; process until well blended.

▲ Substitute your favorite herbed mustard for the country-style Dijon mustard.

Seasoned New Potatoes

1 pound small new potatoes, halved
2 tablespoons butter or margarine
1 tablespoon chopped fresh parsley (optional)
½ teaspoon dried rosemary leaves, crushed (optional)
Dash of pepper

1. Cook potatoes in lightly salted boiling water in medium saucepan 10 minutes or until tender when pierced with fork; drain.
2. Add remaining ingredients; toss lightly to coat.

Makes 4 servings

▲ If small new potatoes are not available, substitute 1 pound larger red-skinned potatoes for new potatoes; cut into quarters before cooking.

Check out the cut-up fresh fruit in your supermarket salad bar for a no-fuss way to "prepare" fruit for last-minute desserts. Add a festive touch with a variety of colors, shapes and textures.

Steamed Broccoli & Carrots

1 pound broccoli
12 baby carrots, peeled
1 tablespoon butter or margarine
Salt and pepper

1. Break broccoli into flowerets. Discard large stems. Trim smaller stems; cut stems into thin slices.

2. Place 2 to 3 inches of water and steamer basket in large saucepan; bring water to a boil.

3. Add broccoli and carrots; cover. Steam 6 minutes or until vegetables are crisp-tender.

4. Place vegetables in serving bowl. Add butter; toss lightly to coat. Season with salt and pepper to taste.
Makes 4 servings

▲ Substitute ½ pound frozen baby carrots *or* ½ pound regular carrots, cut into 2-inch chunks, for baby carrots.

Fruity Shortcake Slices

Yogurt Sauce (recipe follows)
4 pound cake slices
2 cups fruit (any combination of fresh or canned fruit)

1. Preheat broiler.

2. Prepare Yogurt Sauce; cover. Refrigerate.

3. Place cake in shallow baking pan or on rack of broiler pan. Broil 1 to 2 minutes or until lightly toasted; set aside.

4. When ready to serve, place cake slices on individual dessert plates; top with fruit and sauce.
Makes 4 servings

Yogurt Sauce
½ cup sour cream
¼ cup plain yogurt

Combine sour cream and yogurt; mix until well blended.

Top left to bottom right: Fruity Shortcake Slice, Broiled Orange Roughy with Green Peppercorn Sauce (page 67), Seasoned New Potatoes (page 67), Steamed Broccoli & Carrots

Oyster Poor Boys

Cole Slaw Vinaigrette

Orange slices with vanilla yogurt

GAME PLAN

▲ **Prepare Cole Slaw Vinaigrette.**

▲ **Prepare Oyster Poor Boys.**

Oyster Poor Boys

Spicy Mayonnaise
(recipe follows)
¾ cup cornmeal
¼ cup all-purpose flour
½ teaspoon salt
⅛ teaspoon pepper
About ¾ cup vegetable oil for frying
2 pints shucked oysters, drained
4 French bread rolls, split
Lettuce leaves
Tomato slices

1. Prepare Spicy Mayonnaise; cover. Set aside.
2. Combine cornmeal, flour, salt and pepper in shallow bowl; set aside.
3. Heat oil in medium skillet over medium heat. Pat oysters dry with paper towels. Dip oysters into cornmeal mixture to coat.
4. Fry in batches 5 minutes or until golden brown, turning once. Drain on paper towels.
5. Spread rolls with Spicy Mayonnaise; fill with lettuce, tomatoes and oysters.
Makes 4 sandwiches

Spicy Mayonnaise

½ cup mayonnaise
2 tablespoons plain yogurt
¼ teaspoon ground red pepper
1 clove garlic, minced

Combine all ingredients; mix until well blended.

▲ Substitute French bread loaf, split and cut into 4-inch lengths, for French bread rolls.

Cole Slaw Vinaigrette

1 (8-ounce) package cole slaw mix
Vinaigrette
(recipe follows)

1. Place cole slaw mix in medium bowl.
2. Prepare Vinaigrette; pour over cole slaw mix. Toss lightly to coat; cover. Refrigerate.
Makes 4 servings

Vinaigrette

¼ cup vegetable oil
2 tablespoons white wine vinegar
1 tablespoon honey
Salt and pepper

Whisk together oil, vinegar and honey. Season with salt and pepper to taste.

Top left to bottom right:
Cole Slaw Vinaigrette,
Oyster Poor Boy

Salmon, Fettuccine & Cabbage

Sourdough rolls

Make-It-Easy Lemon Tarts

GAME PLAN

▲ **Preheat oven to 450°F.**

▲ **Boil water for fettuccine.**

▲ **Shred cabbage and flake salmon.**

▲ **Prepare and bake tart shells for Make-It-Easy Lemon Tarts.**

▲ **While tart shells are baking, prepare pie filling for dessert.**

▲ **Finish Salmon, Fettuccine & Cabbage.**

▲ **Just before serving, finish dessert.**

Salmon, Fettuccine & Cabbage

1 (9-ounce) package fresh fettuccine
¼ cup plus 2 tablespoons seasoned rice vinegar
2 tablespoons vegetable oil
½ small head of cabbage, shredded (about 7 cups)
½ teaspoon fennel seeds
1 (15½-ounce) can salmon, drained, flaked, bones removed
Salt and pepper

1. Cook fettuccine in lightly salted boiling water according to package directions (about 5 minutes); drain.

2. Heat vinegar and oil in large skillet over medium-high heat. Add cabbage; cook 3 minutes or until crisp-tender, stirring occasionally.

3. Stir in fennel seeds. Add fettuccine; toss lightly to coat. Add salmon; mix lightly.

4. Heat thoroughly, stirring occasionally. Season with salt and pepper to taste. Garnish as desired.

Makes 4 servings

▲ Substitute dried fettuccine for fresh fettuccine.

Make-It-Easy Lemon Tarts

1 (9-inch) refrigerated pie crust
1 package (4-serving size) lemon instant pudding and pie filling (plus ingredients to prepare mix)

1. Preheat oven to 450°F.

2. Cut four (4½-inch) circles from pie crust. Line muffin cups with pastry circles. Prick bottoms and sides with fork.

3. Bake 8 minutes or until lightly browned. Cool.

4. Meanwhile, prepare pie filling according to package directions. Let stand 5 minutes or until thickened; cover. Refrigerate.

5. Just before serving, spoon pie filling into tart shells.

Makes 4 servings

▲ Substitute your favorite flavor canned pie filling for prepared pie filling.

Garlic Shrimp & Vegetables

Cheesy Lahvosh

Spinach Fettuccine

Honey-Glazed Pineapple Slices

GAME PLAN

▲ **Preheat oven to 375°F and boil water for fettuccine.**

▲ **Chop vegetables and mince garlic for Garlic Shrimp & Vegetables.**

▲ **Prepare Cheesy Lahvosh and cook fettuccine.**

▲ **While lahvosh is baking and fettuccine is cooking, finish stir-fry.**

▲ **Finish Spinach Fettuccine.**

▲ **Just before serving, prepare Honey-Glazed Pineapple Slices.**

Top to bottom: Garlic Shrimp & Vegetables with Spinach Fettuccine, Cheesy Lahvosh

Garlic Shrimp & Vegetables

2 tablespoons butter
1 tablespoon olive oil
1 bunch green onions, chopped
1 red pepper, chopped
1 pound peeled, deveined large shrimp
2 cloves garlic, minced
Juice of 1 lime
Salt and pepper

1. Heat butter and oil in medium skillet or wok over medium heat. Add onions and red pepper. Stir-fry 2 minutes or until vegetables are crisp-tender.
2. Add shrimp and garlic; stir-fry 2 minutes or until shrimp turn pink.
3. Stir in lime juice. Season with salt and black pepper to taste. Garnish as desired.
Makes 4 servings

Cheesy Lahvosh

12 small lahvosh (3 inches in diameter)
3 tablespoons butter, melted
¼ cup grated Parmesan cheese

1. Preheat oven to 375°F.
2. Brush lahvosh with butter. Sprinkle with cheese. Place on ungreased baking sheet.
3. Bake 5 minutes or until cheese begins to melt.   *Makes 4 servings*

Spinach Fettuccine

1 (9-ounce) package fresh spinach fettuccine
1 tablespoon butter
1 teaspoon dried basil leaves, crushed (optional)
Salt and pepper

1. Cook fettuccine in lightly salted boiling water according to package directions (about 5 minutes); drain.
2. Combine fettuccine, butter and basil in serving bowl; toss lightly to coat. Season with salt and pepper to taste.
Makes 4 servings

Honey-Glazed Pineapple Slices

1 (20-ounce) can pineapple slices, drained
¼ to ⅓ cup honey
Toasted shredded coconut (optional)

1. Preheat broiler. Position oven rack about 4 inches from heat source.
2. Place pineapple slices on rack of broiler pan. Drizzle honey over pineapple slices.
3. Broil 5 minutes or until honey starts to bubble. Sprinkle with coconut, if desired. Serve warm.
Makes 4 servings

Savory Seafood Soup

French bread

Tossed Green Salad with Buttermilk Dressing

Fruity Cookies & Cream

GAME PLAN

▲ **Prepare Savory Seafood Soup.**

▲ **While bringing vegetable mixture to a boil for soup, prepare greens and slice cucumber for Tossed Green Salad with Buttermilk Dressing (page 78).**

▲ **While vegetables for soup are cooking, assemble salad and prepare dressing.**

▲ **Beat whipping cream, slice strawberries and crumble macaroons for Fruity Cookies & Cream (page 78).**

▲ **Finish soup.**

▲ **Just before serving, finish dessert.**

Savory Seafood Soup

2½ cups water or chicken broth
1½ cups dry white wine
1 small onion, chopped
½ red pepper, chopped
½ green pepper, chopped
1 small clove garlic, minced
½ pound halibut, cut into 1-inch chunks
½ pound sea scallops, halved crosswise
1 teaspoon dried thyme leaves, crushed
Juice of ½ lime
Dash of hot pepper sauce
Salt and black pepper

1. Combine water, wine, onion, red and green peppers and garlic in large saucepan. Bring to a boil.

2. Reduce heat to medium; cover. Cook 15 minutes or until vegetables are tender, stirring occasionally.

3. Add fish, scallops and thyme. Continue cooking 2 minutes or until fish and scallops turn opaque.

4. Stir in lime juice and hot pepper sauce. Season with salt and black pepper to taste.

Makes 4 servings

There are two common varieties of scallops. Bay scallops are tiny scallops that are harvested mainly from the East Coast; they tend to cost more than sea scallops, which are about three times as large. If cut into halves or thirds, sea scallops make an economical alternative to bay scallops.

When purchasing scallops, select those with a creamy white color, a shiny texture and a sweet smell. Scallops that appear to be stark white have been soaked in water and might not be the best buy for your money. Scallops should be used within one day of purchase to guarantee freshness. Cook scallops briefly to prevent overcooking, which tends to toughen them.

Clockwise from top left: Fruity Cookies & Cream (page 78), Tossed Green Salad with Buttermilk Dressing (page 78), Savory Seafood Soup

Add variety to your salads with some of the "exotic" greens that are readily available in the produce section of the supermarket—radicchio and arugula are just a couple of the many newcomers. Each adds its own special color, flavor and texture to a recipe.

Tossed Green Salad with Buttermilk Dressing

Buttermilk Dressing (recipe follows)
6 cups torn mixed greens
½ cucumber, thinly sliced
½ cup pitted ripe olives

1. Prepare Buttermilk Dressing; set aside.
2. Combine greens, cucumber and olives in large salad bowl; toss lightly. Serve with dressing.
Makes 4 servings

Buttermilk Dressing

½ cup mayonnaise
½ cup buttermilk
1 teaspoon white wine vinegar
½ teaspoon green peppercorns, minced (optional)
¼ teaspoon salt

Whisk together all ingredients.

Fruity Cookies & Cream

½ cup whipping cream
1 tablespoon powdered sugar
1 teaspoon vanilla
1 cup green seedless grapes (about ½ pound)
8 strawberries, sliced
4 large macaroons, crumbled

1. Beat whipping cream at high speed with electric mixer until soft peaks form. Add powdered sugar and vanilla; continue beating at high speed until stiff peaks form. Cover; refrigerate.
2. When ready to serve, layer half of the fruit in individual dessert dishes; top with half of the whipped cream mixture.
3. Cover with macaroons and the remaining fruit. Top with the remaining whipped cream mixture.
Makes 4 servings

▲ Substitute 8 small macaroons for 4 large macaroons.

If using large grapes, cut them in half before combining with strawberries.

Easy Eggs, Cheese & Beans

Looking for new ways to include more protein in your diet? Page through this fabulous collection of meatless entrées. If you're in search of a new brunch idea, try Vegetable Frittata. Or dish up Southwest Chili for a terrific one-dish meal. It's all here and more!

Vegetable Frittata (page 80)

EGGS - MENUS

Morning Sparklers
Vegetable Frittata
Melon wedges
Toasted English muffins
(pages 80-81)

▲

Cheesy Fondue
Spinach Salad
Creamy
Chocolate Fondue
(pages 82-83)

▲

Southwest Chili
Cheesy Corn Sticks
Lime sherbet with
fresh fruit
(pages 84-85)

▲

Cinnamon-Toast
Croissants
Garden Omelets
Assorted fresh fruit
(pages 86-87)

▲

Southwestern
Tortilla Stack
Orange Poppy Seed
Salad
Chocolate-Dipped
Strawberries
(pages 88-90)

▲

Bold titles indicate recipes included

Morning Sparklers

Vegetable Frittata

Melon wedges

Toasted English muffins

GAME PLAN

▲ **Prepare Vegetable Frittata.**

▲ **While frittata is cooking, slice melon into wedges and toast English muffins.**

▲ **Just before serving, prepare Morning Sparklers.**

Morning Sparklers

2 (12-ounce) cans strawberry or apricot nectar
2 (10-ounce) bottles carbonated mineral water
Ice

Combine strawberry nectar and mineral water in 2-quart pitcher. Serve over ice.

Makes 6 servings

Vegetable Frittata

1½ tablespoons olive oil, divided
¼ cup chopped onion
6 eggs
1 (10-ounce) package frozen chopped spinach, thawed, drained
¾ cup (3 ounces) shredded Cheddar cheese
½ teaspoon salt
⅛ teaspoon black pepper
Dash of ground red pepper
Dash of ground nutmeg

1. Heat 1 tablespoon of the olive oil in 10-inch skillet over medium heat. Add onion; cook until tender, stirring occasionally. Remove onion from skillet with slotted spoon; set aside.

2. Lightly beat eggs in medium bowl. Add onion, spinach, cheese and seasonings.

3. Heat the remaining 1½ teaspoons oil in same skillet. Add egg mixture. Cook 5 minutes or until bottom is lightly browned.

4. Place large plate over frittata. Invert frittata onto plate. Return frittata, uncooked side down, to skillet.

5. Continue cooking 4 minutes or until set. Cut into wedges to serve. Garnish as desired.

Makes 4 to 6 servings

For best results, press spinach between two nested pie plates, tilting plates over sink to drain well.

Top to bottom: Morning Sparklers, Vegetable Frittata

Cheesy Fondue

Spinach Salad

Creamy Chocolate Fondue

GAME PLAN

▲ **Chop chocolate; prepare fruit (except for banana chunks) and cake dippers for Creamy Chocolate Fondue.**

▲ **Prepare spinach and vegetables for Spinach Salad.**

▲ **Prepare Cheesy Fondue.**

▲ **While heating wine, finish salad.**

▲ **Just before serving, finish dessert.**

Top to bottom: Cheesy Fondue, Spinach Salad

Cheesy Fondue

2 cups (8 ounces) shredded Swiss cheese
2 cups (8 ounces) shredded Monterey Jack cheese
2 tablespoons all-purpose flour
1½ cups dry white wine or apple juice
Dash of ground nutmeg
Dash of ground red pepper
1 French bread loaf, cut into cubes
1 large Granny Smith apple, cut into wedges

1. Combine cheeses and flour; toss lightly to coat.

2. Bring wine to a simmer over medium heat in fondue pot. Gradually add cheeses, stirring constantly, until melted.

3. Stir in nutmeg and pepper. Serve with bread cubes and apple wedges for dipping. Keep warm, stirring occasionally.
Makes 4 servings

Spinach Salad

½ (10-ounce) package fresh spinach, rinsed, stems removed
2 carrots, cut into julienne strips
1 bunch radishes, thinly sliced
Bottled Italian dressing

1. Place spinach in large salad bowl.

2. Add carrots and radishes; toss lightly. Serve with dressing.
Makes 4 servings

Creamy Chocolate Fondue

2 (5-ounce) bars white chocolate with nuts, chopped
¼ cup half-and-half
Strawberries, banana chunks, peeled kiwifruit slices, cookies or pound cake cubes

1. Combine chocolate and half-and-half in small fondue pot or saucepan.

2. Cook over low heat, stirring constantly, until chocolate is melted. Serve warm with fruit, cookies or pound cake for dipping.
Makes 4 servings

Southwest Chili

Cheesy Corn Sticks

Lime sherbet with fresh fruit

GAME PLAN

▲ **Preheat oven to 425°F.**

▲ **Prepare Southwest Chili.**

▲ **While onions for chili are cooking, start to prepare Cheesy Corn Sticks.**

▲ **While chili is simmering, finish corn sticks.**

Southwest Chili

1 tablespoon olive oil
1 large onion, chopped
2 large tomatoes, chopped
1 (4-ounce) can chopped green chilies, undrained
1 tablespoon chili powder
1 teaspoon ground cumin
1 (15-ounce) can red kidney beans, undrained
1 (15-ounce) can Great Northern beans, undrained
¼ cup cilantro leaves, chopped (optional)

1. Heat oil in large saucepan over medium heat. Add onion; cook until tender, stirring occasionally.

2. Stir in tomatoes, chilies, chili powder and cumin. Bring to a boil. Add beans with liquid.

3. Reduce heat to low; cover. Simmer 15 minutes, stirring occasionally. Sprinkle individual servings with cilantro, if desired.
Makes 4 servings

Cheesy Corn Sticks

½ cup all-purpose flour
½ cup cornmeal
2 teaspoons baking powder
¼ teaspoon salt
½ cup milk
1 egg, beaten
3 tablespoons vegetable oil
½ cup (2 ounces) shredded Cheddar cheese

1. Preheat oven to 425°F. Heat cast-iron corn stick pan in oven while preparing batter.

2. Combine flour, cornmeal, baking powder and salt in medium bowl; set aside.

3. Combine milk, egg and oil. Add to dry ingredients, stirring just until moistened.

4. Carefully brush hot pan with additional oil. Spoon batter into prepared pan. Sprinkle batter with cheese.

5. Bake 10 minutes or until lightly browned.
Makes 7 to 9 corn sticks

Top to bottom: Southwest Chili, Cheesy Corn Sticks

Cinnamon-Toast Croissants

Garden Omelets

Assorted fresh fruit

GAME PLAN

▲ **Preheat broiler.**

▲ **Spread croissants with butter; sprinkle with sugar mixture.**

▲ **Prepare Garden Omelets.**

▲ **Just before serving, broil Cinnamon-Toast Croissants.**

Cinnamon-Toast Croissants

¼ cup sugar
1 teaspoon ground cinnamon
2 croissants, halved lengthwise
Butter or margarine, softened

1. Preheat broiler. Position oven rack about 4 inches from heat source.

2. Combine sugar and cinnamon. Lightly spread cut sides of croissants with butter; sprinkle with sugar mixture.

3. Place on baking sheet. Broil until lightly browned.

Makes 2 servings

Garden Omelets

Vegetable Filling (recipe follows)
2 tablespoons butter or margarine, divided
4 eggs, lightly beaten
Salt and pepper

1. Prepare Vegetable Filling; set aside.

2. Melt 1 tablespoon of the butter in 9-inch nonstick skillet over medium heat. Add half of the beaten eggs. Season with salt and pepper to taste. As eggs set, lift slightly with spatula to allow uncooked portion to flow underneath.

3. When eggs are set but top is still moist, place half of the filling on half of omelet.

4. Slip spatula underneath and tip skillet to loosen omelet; gently fold in half. Turn out onto serving plate; keep warm.

5. Repeat with the remaining eggs and filling.

Makes 2 servings

Vegetable Filling

1 tablespoon olive oil
1 zucchini, cut into julienne strips
3 ounces fresh mushrooms, sliced
1 medium tomato, chopped
½ teaspoon dried basil leaves, crushed
¼ teaspoon dried oregano leaves, crushed
Salt and pepper

1. Heat oil in medium skillet over medium heat. Add zucchini, mushrooms, tomato and herbs.

2. Reduce heat to low. Cook until zucchini is crisp-tender and moisture has evaporated. Season with salt and pepper to taste.

Top right to bottom left: Cinnamon-Toast Croissants, Garden Omelets

Southwestern Tortilla Stack

Orange Poppy Seed Salad

Chocolate-Dipped Strawberries

GAME PLAN

▲ **Preheat oven to 425°F.**

▲ **Prepare Chocolate-Dipped Strawberries (page 90).**

▲ **Prepare Southwestern Tortilla Stack.**

▲ **While tortilla stack is baking, prepare Orange Poppy Seed Salad (page 90).**

Southwestern Tortilla Stack

1 (30-ounce) can vegetarian refried beans
½ cup sour cream
1 (4-ounce) can chopped green chilies, drained
½ teaspoon ground cumin
3 (10-inch) flour tortillas
1 cup (4 ounces) shredded Cheddar cheese

1. Preheat oven to 425°F. Grease 10-inch round casserole dish.

2. Combine beans, sour cream, chilies and cumin; set aside.

3. Place one tortilla in bottom of prepared casserole. Top with half of the bean mixture and one third of the cheese. Top with second tortilla; repeat layers of beans and cheese.

4. Cover with remaining tortilla; sprinkle with remaining cheese. Cover.

5. Bake 20 minutes or until thoroughly heated. Cut into wedges. Serve with salsa, if desired.
Makes 4 to 6 servings

Vegetarian refried beans differ from other varieties of refried beans because, as the name implies, they contain no animal by-products. Other varieties of refried beans are often prepared with lard or beef flavoring.

For variety, you can substitute one of the many kinds of refried beans on the market today, which include beans with chorizo sausage, chilies or jalapeños.

Top to bottom: Southwestern Tortilla Stack, Orange Poppy Seed Salad (page 90)

Jicama, often referred to as the "Mexican potato," is a root vegetable with a sweet, nutty flavor. Jicama can be purchased in Mexican markets or in the produce section of most large supermarkets. Cut leftover jicama into julienne strips and use as dippers with your favorite vegetable dip. Its crisp water chestnut-like texture makes it a perfect accompaniment to any creamy dip.

Orange Poppy Seed Salad

Honey & Poppy
    Seed Dressing
    (recipe follows)
Lettuce leaves
2 oranges, peeled,
    sliced crosswise
1 small red onion,
    sliced, separated
    into rings
½ small jicama, cut
    into ½-inch strips

1. Prepare Honey & Poppy Seed Dressing; set aside.
2. Arrange lettuce leaves on serving plates; top with oranges, onion and jicama. Serve with dressing.

Makes 4 servings

Honey & Poppy Seed Dressing

½ cup mayonnaise
¼ cup sour cream or
    plain yogurt
2 tablespoons honey
1 tablespoon lemon
    juice
1 teaspoon poppy
    seeds

Whisk together all ingredients. (Dressing may be thinned with a few tablespoons milk, if desired.)

Chocolate-Dipped Strawberries

6 ounces milk
    chocolate
1 tablespoon
    shortening
1 pint strawberries,
    rinsed and dried
    well

1. Line small tray with waxed paper.
2. In small saucepan over low heat, melt chocolate with shortening, stirring until smooth.
3. Dip tips of strawberries into chocolate. Place on prepared tray. Refrigerate until ready to serve.

Makes 4 servings

Double-Dipped Strawberries:

In addition to milk chocolate, melt 4 ounces white chocolate. After milk chocolate hardens on strawberry, dip tip into white chocolate, leaving some milk chocolate showing.

Stir raisins into any remaining melted chocolate. Drop by spoonfuls onto waxed paper. Refrigerate until set.

EMERGENCY SUBSTITUTIONS

If you don't have:	Use:
1 teaspoon baking powder	1/4 teaspoon baking powder + 1/2 teaspoon cream of tartar
1/2 cup firmly packed brown sugar	1/2 cup granulated sugar mixed with 2 tablespoons molasses
1 cup buttermilk	1 cup plain yogurt *or* 1 tablespoon vinegar or lemon juice plus enough milk to make 1 cup (Stir; let mixture stand 5 minutes.)
1 cup sweetened whipped cream	4 1/2 ounces frozen whipped topping, thawed
1 ounce (1 square) unsweetened chocolate	3 tablespoons unsweetened cocoa + 1 tablespoon shortening
2 ounces (2 squares) semisweet chocolate	2 ounces (about 1/3 cup) semisweet chocolate morsels
1/2 cup corn syrup	1/2 cup granulated sugar + 2 tablespoons water
1 tablespoon cornstarch	2 tablespoons all-purpose flour
1 whole egg	2 egg yolks + 1 tablespoon water *or* 2 egg whites
1 cup sour cream	1 cup plain yogurt
1 clove garlic	1/8 teaspoon garlic powder
1 tablespoon fresh herbs	1 teaspoon dried herbs
1 cup honey	1 1/4 cups granulated sugar + 1/4 cup water
1 teaspoon dry mustard	1 tablespoon prepared mustard
1 small onion	1 teaspoon onion powder *or* 1 tablespoon rehydrated instant minced onion
2 cups tomato sauce	3/4 cup tomato paste + 1 cup water

Index

METRIC CONVERSION CHART

VOLUME MEASUREMENT (dry)

⅛ teaspoon = .5 mL
¼ teaspoon = 1 mL
½ teaspoon = 2 mL
¾ teaspoon = 4 mL
1 teaspoon = 5 mL
1 tablespoon = 15 mL
2 tablespoons = 25 mL
¼ cup = 50 mL
⅓ cup = 75 mL
⅔ cup = 150 mL
¾ cup = 175 mL
1 cup = 250 mL
2 cups = 1 pint = 500 mL
3 cups = 750 mL
4 cups = 1 quart = 1 L

VOLUME MEASUREMENT (fluid)

1 fluid ounce (2 tablespoons) = 30 mL
4 fluid ounces (½ cup) = 125 mL
8 fluid ounces (1 cup) = 250 mL
12 fluid ounces (1½ cups) = 375 mL
16 fluid ounces (2 cups) = 500 mL

WEIGHT (MASS)

½ ounce = 15 g
1 ounce = 30 g
3 ounces = 85 g
3.75 ounces = 100 g
4 ounces = 115 g
8 ounces = 225 g
12 ounces = 340 g
16 ounces = 1 pound = 450 g

DIMENSION

1/16 inch = 2 mm
⅛ inch = 3 mm
¼ inch = 6 mm
½ inch = 1.5 cm
¾ inch = 2 cm
1 inch = 2.5 cm

OVEN TEMPERATURES

250°F = 120°C
275°F = 140°C
300°F = 150°C
325°F = 160°C
350°F = 180°C
375°F = 190°C
400°F = 200°C
425°F = 220°C
450°F = 230°C

BAKING PAN SIZES

Utensil	Inches/ Quarts	Metric Volume	Centimeters
Baking or	8×8×2	2 L	20×20×5
Cake pan	9×9×2	2.5 L	22×22×5
(square or	12×8×2	3 L	30×20×5
rectangular)	13×9×2	3.5 L	33×23×5
Loaf Pan	8×4×3	1.5 L	20×10×7
	9×5×3	2 L	23×13×7
Round Layer	8×1½	1.2 L	20×4
Cake Pan	9×1½	1.5 L	23×4
Pie Plate	8×1¼	750 mL	20×3
	9×1¼	1 L	23×3
Baking Dish	1 quart	1 L	
or	1½ quart	1.5 L	
Casserole	2 quart	2 L	